learn to
paint
and
draw

learn to
paint
and
draw

A complete guide to drawing
and painting techniques

p

This is a Parragon book
This edition published in 2005

Parragon
Queen Street House
4 Queen Street
Bath BA1 1HE,UK

Copyright © Parragon 2003

Designed, produced and packaged by
Stonecastle Graphics Limited

Drawings by Terry Longhurst
Text by Angela Gair

All rights reserved. No part of this publication may be
reproduced, stored in a retrieval system, or transmitted
in any way or by any means, electronic, mechanical,
photocopying, recording or otherwise, without the
prior permission of the copyright holder.

ISBN 1-40545-627-2

Printed in China

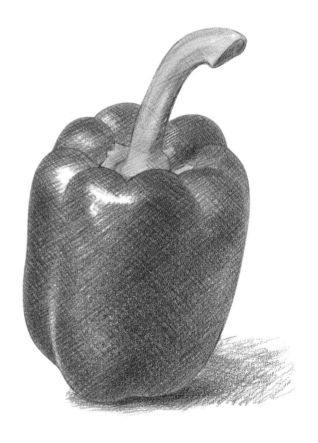

CONTENTS

INTRODUCTION

Drawing is instant art. It is the most immediate means of recording not only what you see but your emotional response to it. A simple pencil or a piece of charcoal is like an extension of your fingers: with it you can jot down ideas, impressions and images at a moment's notice. Some of the most beautiful drawings in the world – Rembrandt's pen-and-ink sketches, for example – succeed in capturing life and movement, emotion, mood and atmosphere with just the briefest of outlines on paper.

Nevertheless, there is a perception that there is something 'clever' or 'difficult' about drawing, that the ability to draw is something one is either born with or not. This may be true to a certain extent, but drawing is just like any other creative manual skill, like gardening or cooking – the fact that you are interested in the subject at all suggests that you have some facility for it. All you need is the patience to learn the fundamental techniques, be it how to prune a rose, how to make a béchamel sauce – or how to draw a figure in proportion.

Once you have grasped the fundamentals, you will have the confidence to allow your natural creativity to take over and you can begin to forge your own path, bend the rules a little, discover your own unique way of representing the world.

In this book you will find an introduction to the materials, marks and effects which can be achieved with a wide variety of drawing media. You will also find explained, simply and clearly, some of the underlying principles of drawing: tone and colour, composition, perspective and so on. These are all 'learnable' principles which, once mastered, will enable you to tackle any subject with confidence and enthusiasm. I hope the book will help you to discover your hidden artistic talents and inspire you to draw, draw, draw.

Learning to draw gives you a wide choice of materials, most of which are easily obtainable and relatively inexpensive. However, if you are just starting out it may be wise to begin with a simple pencil or pen. Eventually, as your confidence grows, you will want to experiment with different media and techniques. The following pages will introduce you to the various drawing media, both monochrome and colour, and give you an idea of their expressive potential.

Getting Started

In this section you will learn about composition, perspective, tone and colour, which are essential to the success of any kind of painting or drawing. An understanding of these will help you to achieve the results you want much more easily and to increase the expressiveness of your drawings. There is also an introduction to the range of materials you can use.

PENCILS AND CHARCOAL

Pencils and charcoal are traditionally used for making sketches and preliminary studies but they can also be used for highly finished drawings that are works of art in their own right.

Drawing pencils come in several grades, 'H' denoting hard and 'B' denoting soft. The HB (medium grade) is a good all-rounder, while an 8B (very soft) will give you a wide range of linear and tonal effects. Hard leads are suitable for precise lines and details, but in general they are less versatile than the soft leads.

The pencil is the most familiar, natural drawing instrument. It is also the most versatile, capable of producing an infinite range of lines and marks. Pencil drawings can be done using lines alone, or by using tone alone without lines, or any number of techniques in between. The quality of a pencil line can be varied by the grade of pencil chosen, its sharpness, the way it is held, the degree of pressure applied, and the texture of the paper surface.

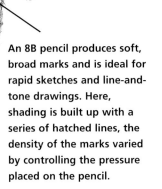

An 8B pencil produces soft, broad marks and is ideal for rapid sketches and line-and-tone drawings. Here, shading is built up with a series of hatched lines, the density of the marks varied by controlling the pressure placed on the pencil.

This artichoke head was drawn with a 2B pencil with a blunt point. By holding the pencil almost parallel with the paper and hatching with the side of the lead, rather than the point, you can create soft and subtle areas of tone.

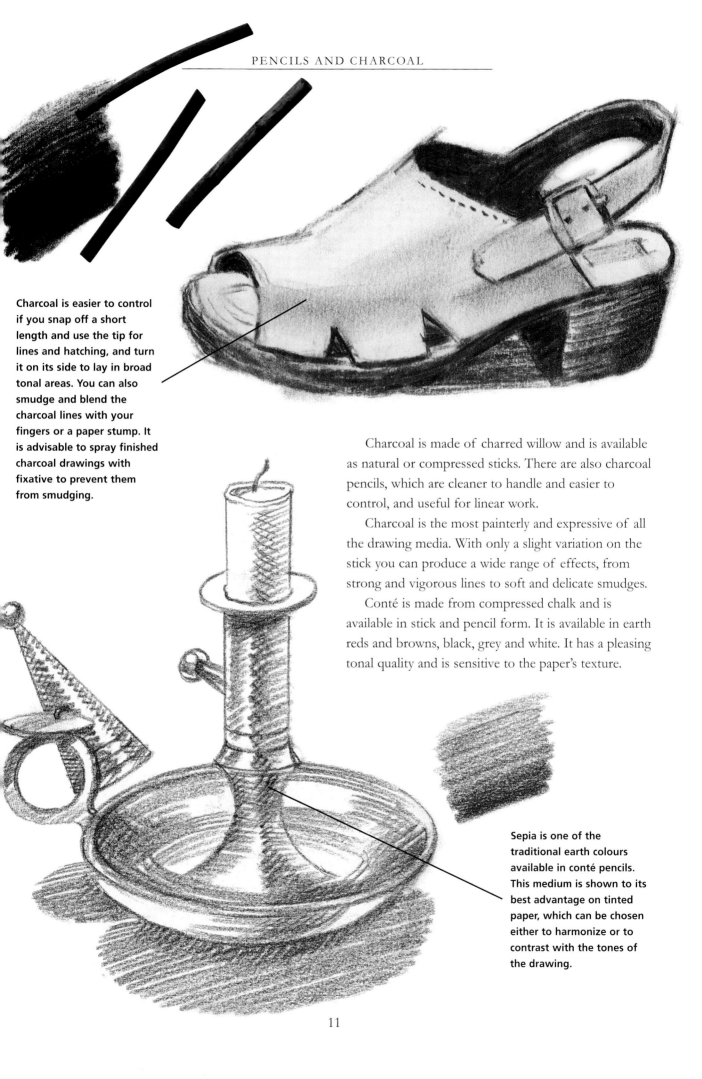

Charcoal is easier to control if you snap off a short length and use the tip for lines and hatching, and turn it on its side to lay in broad tonal areas. You can also smudge and blend the charcoal lines with your fingers or a paper stump. It is advisable to spray finished charcoal drawings with fixative to prevent them from smudging.

Charcoal is made of charred willow and is available as natural or compressed sticks. There are also charcoal pencils, which are cleaner to handle and easier to control, and useful for linear work.

Charcoal is the most painterly and expressive of all the drawing media. With only a slight variation on the stick you can produce a wide range of effects, from strong and vigorous lines to soft and delicate smudges.

Conté is made from compressed chalk and is available in stick and pencil form. It is available in earth reds and browns, black, grey and white. It has a pleasing tonal quality and is sensitive to the paper's texture.

Sepia is one of the traditional earth colours available in conté pencils. This medium is shown to its best advantage on tinted paper, which can be chosen either to harmonize or to contrast with the tones of the drawing.

PEN AND INK

Beginners are often afraid of drawing with pen and ink because mistakes can't be rubbed out. But ink is actually a very flexible and expressive medium, and well worth trying out.

Drawing pens fall into two categories: dip pens and reservoir pens. The traditional reed, quill and steel-nibbed pens are classified as dip pens, as they are loaded by being dipped directly into the ink. These pens produce lively, animated lines which vary according to the speed of line and the amount of pressure on the nib. Reservoir pens include fountain pens, felt-tips, fibre-tips, technical pens and even the humble ballpoint. They produce uniform, less giving lines but they are convenient as they contain their own supply of ink. Experiment with different pens and nibs to discover which suits you best.

Drawing inks come in black and a range of colours. Waterproof inks, such as Indian ink, dry to a hard, glossy film so that washes can be laid on top. Water-soluble ink can be spread by washing areas of the drawing with a wet brush.

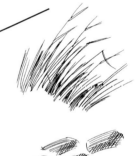

An incredible variety of lines and marks can be made with pen and ink. As well as lines, you can also build up tone and texture with short strokes, scribbles and dots. Be bold: fast lines are truer and more expressive than hesitant ones.

This sketchbook drawing of a Greek smallholding was made with a dip pen and black Indian ink. The major shapes of the subject were sketched in with free-flowing lines and then, using a loose hatching technique, shading was added. The feeling of strong sunlight is depicted through the contrast of white paper and densely hatched shadow tones.

Techniques

To begin with it is a good idea to sketch in the composition lightly with faint pencil lines and then work over them ink. As you gain confidence you will enjoy making spontaneous drawings directly in ink.

The traditional method of building up a tonal drawing with a pen is by hatching and cross-hatching.

Another, freer method of achieving tonal effects is to combine drawing in ink with washes of diluted ink. It is best to use a smooth, hard-surfaced paper when drawing with pen and ink; on absorbent papers the ink line may blur and bleed.

Dense tones can be built up by cross-hatching in multiple directions. The effects produced by cross-hatching can be varied by changing the angle of the intersecting lines, and subtle gradations in tone can be achieved by varying the line density.

A fine-point black felt-tip pen on smooth cartridge paper was used for this still-life drawing. Light and shade and even 'colour' are suggested using line rather than tone. Fine parallel lines are drawn where the tones are lightest; these are cross-hatched once for the mid-tones and twice for the dark tones.

Pen lines can be combined with ink washes applied with a soft brush – a technique known as line-and-wash. The outlines were drawn with a dip pen and ink over a light pencil drawing. When dry, the tonal areas were built up with overlaid washes of diluted grey-blue ink. The final details were added on top with pen and ink.

DRAWING WITH COLOUR

When the vast choice of drawing techniques is supplemented by colour, the creative possibilities are endless. Colour can be used not only to describe objects but also to suggest mood and atmosphere.

The colour wheel (right) will help you to understand how colour works and enable you to use it expressively in your drawings. The core colours are the three primaries – red, yellow and blue – so called because they cannot be mixed from other colours. These are linked by the secondary colours, which are each mixed from two primaries: red and yellow make orange, yellow and blue make green, red and blue make violet.

Colours that are next to each other on the wheel are described as harmonious because they share a common base colour. Harmonious colours create a unified image with no jarring notes. Pairs of colours that are opposite each other on the wheel are known as complementary pairs. When placed side by side they intensify each other; thus a patch of red looks more vibrant when juxtaposed with green.

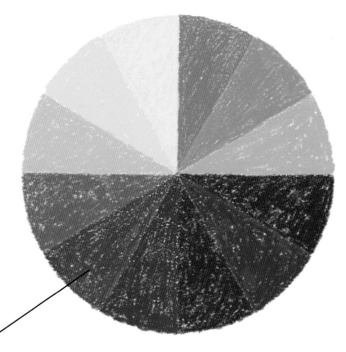

Colours that lie opposite each other on the colour wheel are called complementary colours. When a colour and its complementary are placed next to each other they intensify each other; when mixed together they neutralize each other.

The colour wheel is a simplified version of the colours of the spectrum, formed into a circle. It is a handy reference for understanding the way colours relate to each other. The arrangement of colours on the wheel shows the relationship between the primary colours and their opposite, or complementary colours, and their adjacent colours.

The intense colour of these clementines is brought out using water-soluble pencils. When brushed with water the colour pigment dissolves and spreads to make watercolour-like washes. This technique works best on a slightly textured surface such as watercolour paper.

One half of the wheel comprises warm colours – reds, oranges and yellows – and the other comprises cool blues, greens and violets. Because warm colours appear to advance and cool colours to recede, the use of warm hues in the foreground and cool ones in the background accentuates the illusion of depth and atmosphere in landscape drawings.

Creating colour

With pastels and coloured pencils you can't mix colours together in the way you do paints, but you can use optical and broken-colour mixing techniques that produce exciting effects. Colours can be applied next to or over each other and smoothly blended, or hatched and cross-hatched to create a shimmering web of colour. With pastels you can lay down a patch of colour and then lightly scumble over it with another, creating a 'veil' of colour that partially obscures the under layer. Because the colours mix in the eye, they appear more vibrant.

Soft pastels are very versatile in that they can be both a drawing and a painting medium. By using both the tip and the side of the stick you can produce vigorous lines and powdery 'washes' of colour. In landscape drawings, blended pastel tones are perfect for suggesting the amorphous nature of skies, water and foliage and the fleeting effects of light and weather.

Oil pastels offer intense, vibrant hues and make thick, buttery strokes. Use them for bold, uninhibited statements of pure colour. This sketch shows the effect of complementary contrasts – the cool blues and greens of the background intensify the hot oranges and reds of the sunflower.

SKETCHING WITH PAINTS

*Watercolour and acrylic paints are ideal media for colour sketching
outdoors because they dry quickly and the few materials required to
use them are easily packed into a small shoulder bag.*

Fluid washes of watercolour or thinned acrylic paint
can be used to introduce colour and tone to line
work in pencil, coloured pencil or pen and ink. They
are especially effective for on-the-spot sketches of the
landscape: fast and fluid, they capture the freshness and
spontaneity of the subject.

What you will need

Watercolour equipment is tailor-made for sketching
outdoors – light and easy to carry. A box of dry pan
paints will be lighter than tubes and the inside of the lid
provides a mixing palette. A single brush is all you
need: a good quality brush will hold plenty of paint for
washes and come to a fine point for details. If you are
using a sketchbook, make sure the paper is thick
enough to take a wash: anything less than 300gsm
(140lb) will buckle when wet washes are applied.

Acrylics are great for experimenting with different
techniques when out sketching. Diluted with water they

**When thinned with water,
acrylic paints can be used in
the same way as watercolour.
They dry quickly and are
insoluble when dry; this
means you can apply
successive washes without
muddying those underneath.**

**All you need to paint this
landscape sketch is a piece of
watercolour paper with a
slight 'tooth', a pencil, a
sketchers' pocket box of
watercolours, a medium-size
round brush, a bottle of
water and a water pot. Start
by lightly sketching out the
composition in pencil.**

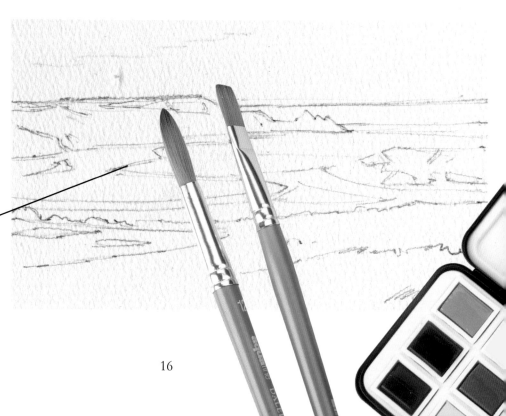

can be used like watercolour; used thickly they produce effects just like oil paints – but they dry much faster. All you need is a select number of tubes and brushes, some heavy paper or a canvas board and a container of water.

Using the traditional watercolour technique of working from light to dark, establish the basic forms and local colours with thin, broad washes. Keep your paints fluid and transparent: this allows light to reflect off the white paper, which is what gives a watercolour its characteristic luminosity.

Apply the mid-tones, then the darkest tones, waiting for each area to dry before you add another wash. Keeping additional painting to a minimum and leaving much of the base wash visible gives the finished sketch a pleasing harmony.

DRAWING SIMPLE SHAPES

The most basic forms to be found in nature – the cube, the sphere, the cone and the cylinder – can be used to simplify your understanding of any object you draw, no matter how complex.

When you come to draw complicated subjects – the human figure, buildings and trees in a landscape, fruits and flowers in a still life – it helps to visualize them first as simple geometric shapes. All the objects around us are combinations of the curves and planes found in the sphere, the cone, the cylinder and the cube. A building is basically a cube; most fruits and vegetables are roughly spherical; a bottle and a tree trunk are basically cylinders; poplar trees are conical in shape, as are some flower heads. Learning to see objects in terms of simple shapes, which can then be broken down into smaller, more complex shapes, helps us to draw them more easily and accurately.

The difference between flat, two-dimensional shapes and solid, three-dimensional forms is the way light falls on objects, creating shadows, half-tones and highlights that reveal their planes and surfaces. In drawing, this is represented using tone and shading – in other words, degrees of light and dark.

These four geometric shapes are the main basic forms to be found in nature and can be used to simplify your understanding of any subject, from a flower to a human figure.

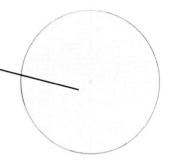

Any shape in nature, from a flower right up to a mountain, can be worked out in simple three-dimensional terms. It was the great artist Cézanne who said, "Treat nature in terms of the cylinder, the sphere, the cone…"

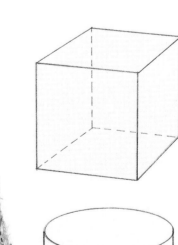

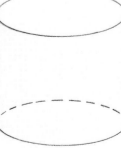

Many vegetables and fruits are spherical in shape and tone and shading in your drawing will help to create the illusion of a solid object.

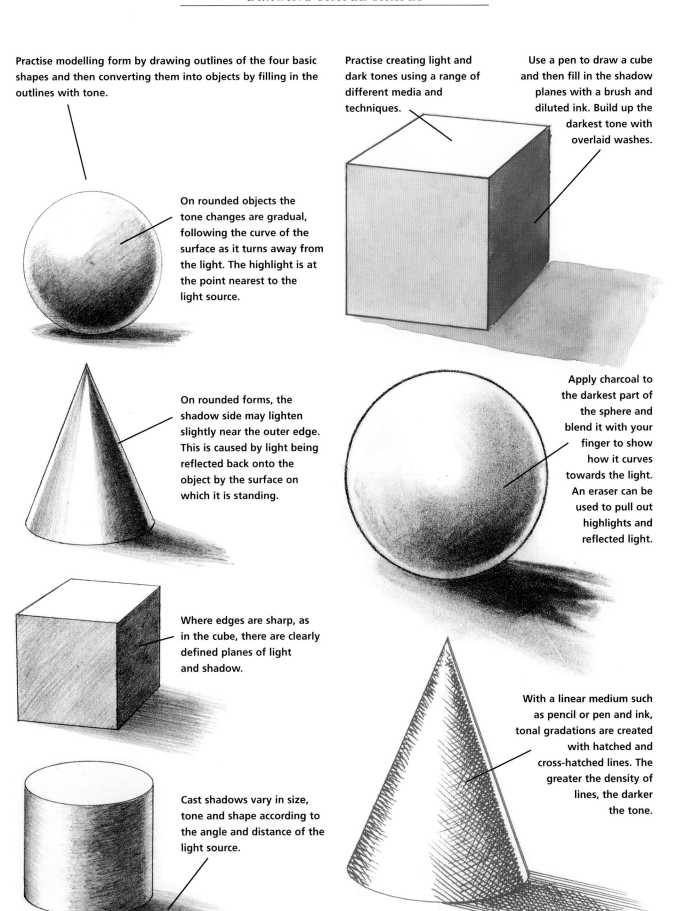

Practise modelling form by drawing outlines of the four basic shapes and then converting them into objects by filling in the outlines with tone.

Practise creating light and dark tones using a range of different media and techniques.

Use a pen to draw a cube and then fill in the shadow planes with a brush and diluted ink. Build up the darkest tone with overlaid washes.

On rounded objects the tone changes are gradual, following the curve of the surface as it turns away from the light. The highlight is at the point nearest to the light source.

On rounded forms, the shadow side may lighten slightly near the outer edge. This is caused by light being reflected back onto the object by the surface on which it is standing.

Apply charcoal to the darkest part of the sphere and blend it with your finger to show how it curves towards the light. An eraser can be used to pull out highlights and reflected light.

Where edges are sharp, as in the cube, there are clearly defined planes of light and shadow.

With a linear medium such as pencil or pen and ink, tonal gradations are created with hatched and cross-hatched lines. The greater the density of lines, the darker the tone.

Cast shadows vary in size, tone and shape according to the angle and distance of the light source.

FORM AND MODELLING

Having learned how to draw simple shapes and use light and shade
to make them look three-dimensional, it is now time to put your
skills to the test and draw a real object.

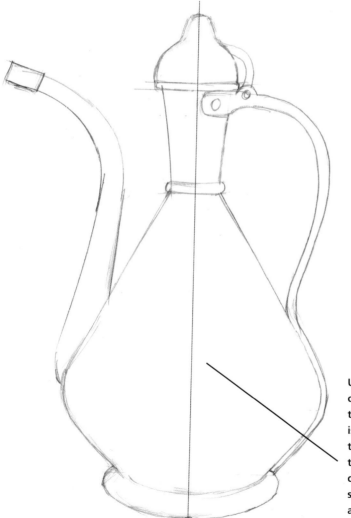

As an introduction to modelling form with tone, start with a pencil drawing of a single object. Search your home for a rounded object such as a vase or jug, preferably without any distracting pattern or texture on it. This Turkish vessel, made of pewter, is an ideal subject because it is a simple yet attractive shape.

Place your subject on a table near a window, or position a lamp to one side of it; this will create a clear

Use a soft pencil to make a careful outline drawing of the vessel. Its bulbous shape is quite tricky: you will find that drawing a line down the centre makes it easier to check the shapes on either side and ensure that they are symmetrical.

You can now rub out the centre line and begin shading. Starting from the left-hand side, use the flat side of the pencil to make long, angled strokes. Leave the patches of highlight white. Fill in the curved brass handle with short strokes of a yellow coloured pencil.

Accentuate the sweeping curves of the handle by working over the shadowed parts with your pencil. This also dulls the yellow and helps to make it look more like brass.

pattern of lights, darks and mid-tones that help to explain form. Observe the way the light falls on the object and make a drawing of it in soft pencil, shading with hatched lines to build up gradually from the lightest tones to the darkest.

If you find it hard to gauge the relative tonal values, try squinting at your subject through half-closed eyes. This has the effect of reducing colour and detail and making the light and dark parts easier to discern.

This is a very important lesson and you will find it worthwhile to make several drawings of the same object, changing the direction of the light and experimenting with different media and ways of shading. You might try blending with charcoal, for instance, or building up tonal washes with ink.

The smooth marks and varied tones produced by charcoal are ideally suited to tonal drawing. Convey the heavy, solid quality of this old-fashioned flat iron by accentuating the quite sharp divisions between one area of tone and another.

Build up to the darkest tones with increasingly dense hatching, leaving the soft highlight on the body of the vessel lighter in tone. Note how the left side is darkest because it is further from the light source, and how the spout darkens as it curves downward. Use heavier strokes where the form curves under at the base.

CONTOUR SHAPES

An outline is a flat shape that describes only two dimensions.
A contour drawing describes all three dimensions – length, width and
depth – because it follows the bumps and hollows within the form.

Drawing most often involves using line to describe the three-dimensional quality of an object. The line must describe the bulk of the form and not just its outline. If you draw the outline of a figure, for example, it looks flat, like a cartoon character. There is no information in the drawing to tell us that the arms, legs and so on are actually rounded. But as soon as you work across the drawing with a few simple contour lines that describe the bumps and hollows created by the bones and muscles, the way the hair lies, and the creases in the clothing, the figure becomes solid and three-dimensional – even without shading.

A contour drawing is rather like a contour map: it travels across the forms, indicating where the surface of the object is closer to us or further away, where it is curved and where it is flat. By making subtle changes in the width and weight of the lines you can also describe the fullness and 'weight' of the forms.

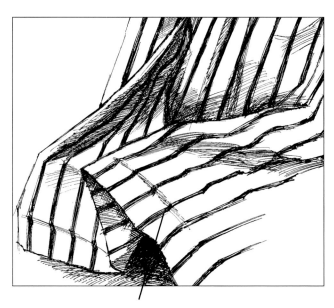

If you drape a piece of striped fabric and then draw it by copying the stripes, you will see how the stripes become contour lines that describe the three-dimensional curves and folds in the fabric.

A pen was used to draw only the outlines of these apples. The drawing conveys very little information about the three-dimensional qualities of the forms, so they look flat.

Here, contour lines are introduced which map out the curvature of the apples, explaining their forms.

The best way to describe objects accurately and make them look convincingly three-dimensional is to draw them as though they are transparent. By drawing both what is seen and what is hidden, you don't just describe the outer shape of an object; you get a better sense of its underlying structure and this helps you to draw it more accurately. You can rub out any unwanted lines later if you want to, though they often add 'texture' to a drawing.

This method is especially useful when drawing cylindrical objects like cups, bowls and vases. If you draw the entire base of the object, and not just the bit you can see at the front, it will appear solid and planted squarely on the surface. You will find it much easier to draw the elliptical shape of the opening accurately, too.

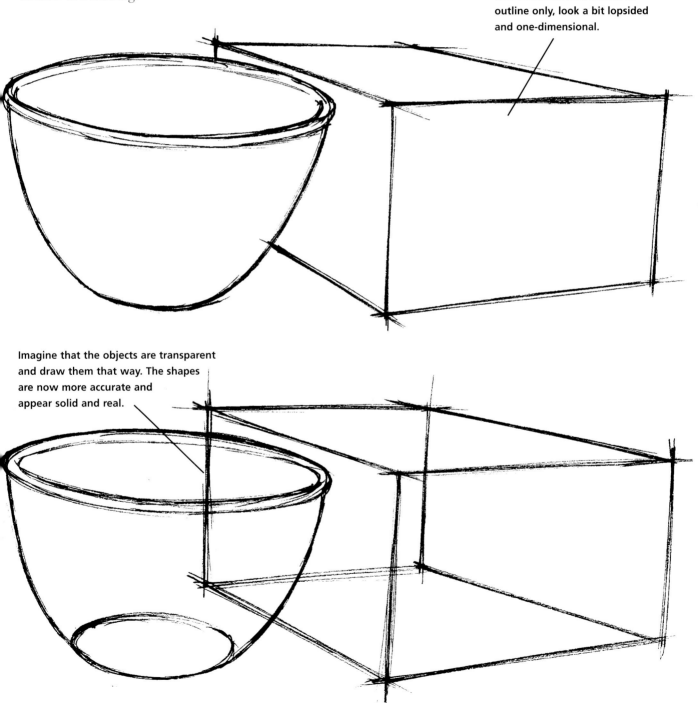

This bowl and box, drawn in outline only, look a bit lopsided and one-dimensional.

Imagine that the objects are transparent and draw them that way. The shapes are now more accurate and appear solid and real.

MODELLING FORM WITH COLOUR

*Modelling with colour means rendering the effects of light and shade
on coloured objects to make them appear solid and real. Experiment
with different ways of mixing and blending colours to create form.*

With coloured drawing media, mixed hues and
tones are created mainly by layering or
interweaving the drawn marks to create the gradations
of tone or colour that model three-dimensional form.

Hatching and cross-hatching

These are the most commonly used methods of creating
blocks of colour and tone with a linear medium such as
coloured pencil. In hatching, closely spaced parallel
lines give the effect of tone; in cross-hatching, the lines
criss-cross to create a fine mesh of denser tone. Simply
by varying the number of lines, their thickness and the

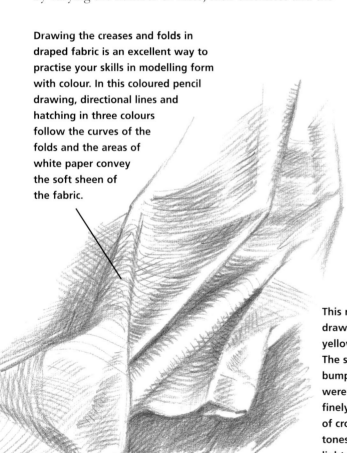

Drawing the creases and folds in
draped fabric is an excellent way to
practise your skills in modelling form
with colour. In this coloured pencil
drawing, directional lines and
hatching in three colours
follow the curves of the
folds and the areas of
white paper convey
the soft sheen of
the fabric.

Do you get confused between colour and
tone when drawing three-dimensional
objects? It helps to sort out the tones
first by doing a monochrome drawing
in pencil or charcoal. Once you've
established the pattern of lights and
darks, you can translate these in
your colour drawing.

This realistic pepper was
drawn with red and
yellow coloured pencils.
The smooth curves,
bumps and dimples
were modelled with a
finely controlled network
of cross-hatched lines, the
tones built up slowly from
light to dark.

For this line-and-wash drawing, start by drawing the subject lightly in pencil. When you are satisfied with the shapes, go over the drawn lines with a dip pen and black waterproof ink.

Now you are ready to apply watercolour washes over your drawing using a soft brush. Squeeze your colours into the wells of a mixing palette and dilute them with water to make pale tints. Leaving areas of the paper bare for the brightest highlights, first apply washes over the bottle, then the tray and glasses. Leave the drawing to dry.

Look for the darkest areas of the subject and build them up gradually with overlaid washes of watercolour, letting each wash dry before adding the next. Leave to dry, then use the pen and black ink to suggest the pattern on the tray and the lettering on the wine bottle label. The pen and ink lines give detail and structure to the objects, while the broad washes of watercolour provide mass and tone that describe their three-dimensional forms.

distance between them, it is possible to obtain infinitely subtle gradations of tone from light to dark. The strokes can be straight or curved, and can be worked in different directions to follow the changing planes and curves in describing solid form.

Shading and blending

With a powdery medium like pastel, graded tones can be achieved by blending together adjacent colours on the surface of the paper. You can blend by rubbing with your fingers, a paper stump or a cotton bud.

Colour washes

Transparent washes of diluted ink or watercolour can be applied layer upon layer with a brush to build up colour and form, as in the pen-and-wash drawing on this page. Gradations of colour and tone are made either by over-working with the same hue to darken a tone or by adding a dark colour over a light one.

SIMPLE PERSPECTIVE

Perspective is a system used by artists to create a convincing illusion
of three-dimensional form and space on a flat piece of paper.
The basic principles are very straightforward.

Before you can draw anything in perspective you must first establish the horizon line. If you can't see the actual horizon (in a town, for instance), just remember that the horizon is at your own eye level. The horizon level will change according to whether you are sitting down or standing up but it is always directly in front of your eyes.

Vanishing points

The basic assumption of perspective is that parallel horizontal lines that recede into the distance appear to converge at a single point on the horizon, at the centre of vision. This is called the vanishing point. All lines above your eye level will slant down to the vanishing point and lines below your eye level will slant up to the vanishing point. This is illustrated in the drawing of a

Two-point perspective
Each side of this house is seen at an angle of roughly 45 degrees to the picture plane. Each side appears to recede towards a vanishing point on the horizon line on the left and right of the image. To draw the building, start with the nearest vertical line and assess the angles at which the sides of the building recede from it. Extend these lines to the vanishing points. Using this framework you can now draw the windows and doors in perspective.

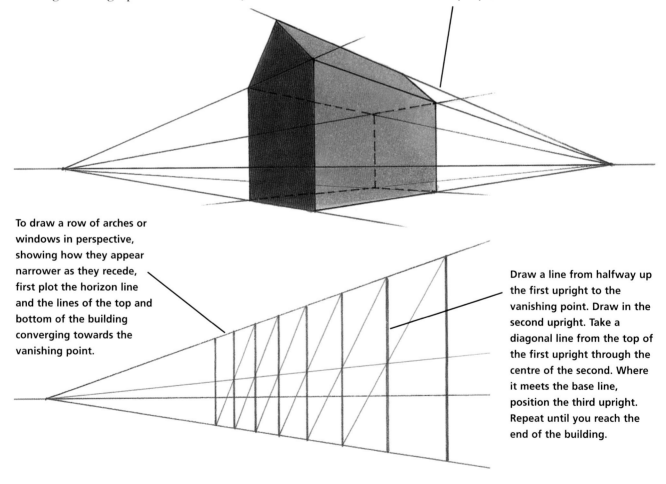

To draw a row of arches or windows in perspective, showing how they appear narrower as they recede, first plot the horizon line and the lines of the top and bottom of the building converging towards the vanishing point.

Draw a line from halfway up the first upright to the vanishing point. Draw in the second upright. Take a diagonal line from the top of the first upright through the centre of the second. Where it meets the base line, position the third upright. Repeat until you reach the end of the building.

bridge below. Standing at one end of the bridge and facing the opposite end, the vanishing point is near the centre of the picture and all receding lines converge to meet at this point.

One- and two-point perspective

One-point perspective refers to a situation where there is only one vanishing point at the centre line of vision. However, objects are often viewed from an oblique angle; if you are drawing the corner of a building, for instance, you would need to plot two vanishing points, at which the converging lines of each side of the building meet.

With two-point perspective it is likely that at least one vanishing point, and sometimes both, will be outside the picture area. You have to imagine the vanishing points in the space beyond your page and estimate the angles of the building by eye.

Objects of equal height look smaller the further away they are. Equally spaced objects also appear closer together as they recede into the distance. Look at the struts and the railway sleepers in this drawing.

When drawing figures which are receding into the distance, plot converging lines from the nearest figure to the vanishing point. You can then draw the distant figures to the correct size in relation to the foreground figure.

AERIAL PERSPECTIVE AND VIEWPOINT

Aerial perspective is a further development of linear perspective. It is based on the idea that what is near to you can be seen in sharper detail than what is in the distance.

The most effective means of creating the illusion of depth in your drawings, particularly in landscapes, is by using tone and colour to recreate the effects of aerial perspective. This term describes a natural optical illusion caused by the presence of water vapour and dust particles in the atmosphere. These affect visibility, making colours, tones and forms appear less distinct the further away they are.

Imagine that you are standing in a field with the landscape stretching away as far as the eye can see. As your eye travels from the foreground to the horizon you will notice that colours which appear warm and bright close up gradually become cooler, paler and

A useful tip for representing the effects of aerial perspective in monochrome is to visualize the landscape almost as a series of vertical, receding planes. The foreground plane is strongest in tone and detail; the middle ground and background planes become progressively paler and less distinct as they get closer to the horizon.

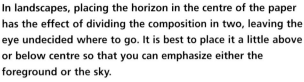

In landscapes, placing the horizon in the centre of the paper has the effect of dividing the composition in two, leaving the eye undecided where to go. It is best to place it a little above or below centre so that you can emphasize either the foreground or the sky.

bluer as they recede towards the horizon. Tones and tonal contrasts appear strongest in the foreground and become progressively weaker in the distance. Texture and detail also become less distinct the further away they are. To create the illusion of deep space in your landscape drawings, all you have to do is to mimic these effects, making your tones and colours fade gradually towards the horizon.

Placing the horizon

It is worth taking time to observe your subject from different viewpoints and to make several sketches of it. You will be surprised how even small changes of viewpoint can dramatically alter the perspective and the impression of depth in the scene. The sketches on this page show the same subject seen from different viewpoints, each creating a very different sense of space. Notice the dramatic effect created by placing the horizon either very high or very low.

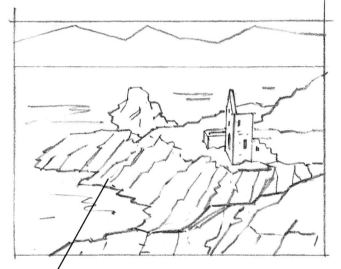

An imaginative viewpoint can make for a more striking image. Looking at the landscape from a high viewpoint is fascinating because it is relatively unfamiliar. Why not climb up to the top of a hill and sketch the scene rolled out before you.

Looking at a scene from a low viewpoint also offers a fresh perspective on the landscape. If you position yourself at the bottom of a slope, for instance, a building at the top of the slope will tower dramatically above the horizon line.

THE ART OF COMPOSITION

When you begin a drawing, the first thing to consider is the composition. Your aim is to achieve the maximum visual impact by dividing the picture space in a balanced, satisfying way.

The underlying geometry of a picture can be compared to the foundations of a building: without this framework the whole thing would collapse.

If a landscape scene is divided symmetrically, with a centrally placed horizon or tree, for instance, the effect could be dull and boring as the composition would tend to fall into two equal halves. In general, dividing the picture area into unequal sections is a reliable way to establish a pleasing composition. Many landscape pictures, for example, are divided into one-third sky, two-thirds land (or vice versa); no one quite knows why, but the human eye finds that this proportion has a pleasing balance.

The drawings below demonstrate a traditional method of dividing up the picture area to achieve a balanced design. The 'rule of thirds' is a simple mathematical formula based on the principles of harmony and proportion. Imagine the picture area divided into thirds, horizontally and vertically; any strong horizontal or vertical elements in the drawing should coincide with these lines and the points where two lines intersect are good places to locate the focal point of the drawing.

Here we have a portrait format picture, again divided into horizontal and vertical thirds. The vase sits on the intersecting vertical on the right and the flowers fall mostly within the upper horizontal third, balanced by the bowls of fruit in the lower third.

This landscape format drawing is divided horizontally and vertically into thirds. Both the jug and the vase of flowers align with the vertical thirds. The points where objects overlap, such as the vase and bowls, are positioned close to where lines intersect.

Balance in a composition should not mean boredom! Elements of exactly equal shape, distance or appearance have a tendency to appear monotonous.

Arrangements based on an underlying geometric shape break up the picture in a pleasing way. Here, a still life is loosely grouped within the shape of an equilateral triangle. This construction has a natural stability, enhanced by grouping the objects so that they overlap each other.

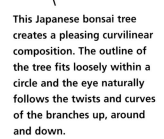

This Japanese bonsai tree creates a pleasing curvilinear composition. The outline of the tree fits loosely within a circle and the eye naturally follows the twists and curves of the branches up, around and down.

The objects in this watercolour still life have been carefully chosen and arranged to create a pleasing composition. It contains related shapes which echo each other and maintain the harmony and unity of the design, while contrasts of shape, tone and colour provide variety and interest.

COMPOSING A PICTURE

The first steps you take in planning a drawing in your mind's eye are vital. The key to this is the composition – having a clearly worked out structure for the image you want to create.

Good composition means arranging the elements in your subject to create an appealing and well-balanced drawing that attracts and holds the viewer's attention. In essence, this means deciding what is to be the centre of interest, where to place it and how to guide the eye towards it in the most interesting way possible.

If you haven't got a viewfinder you can improvise one by arranging your fingers and thumbs into a rectangular shape, as shown. Move your 'frame' closer or further away from one eye, looking at a larger or smaller section of the view, until you find the one you want.

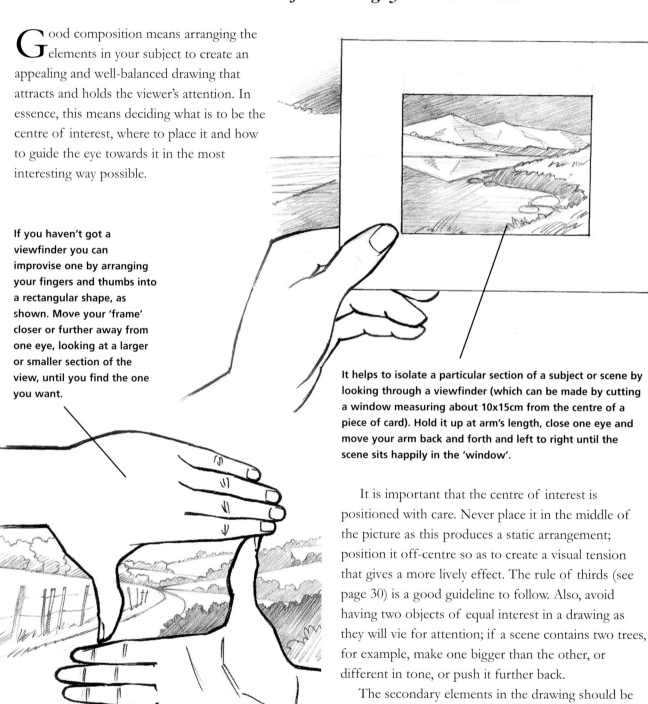

It helps to isolate a particular section of a subject or scene by looking through a viewfinder (which can be made by cutting a window measuring about 10x15cm from the centre of a piece of card). Hold it up at arm's length, close one eye and move your arm back and forth and left to right until the scene sits happily in the 'window'.

It is important that the centre of interest is positioned with care. Never place it in the middle of the picture as this produces a static arrangement; position it off-centre so as to create a visual tension that gives a more lively effect. The rule of thirds (see page 30) is a good guideline to follow. Also, avoid having two objects of equal interest in a drawing as they will vie for attention; if a scene contains two trees, for example, make one bigger than the other, or different in tone, or push it further back.

The secondary elements in the drawing should be arranged so as to take the eye on a gentle journey from foreground to background, or from one object to

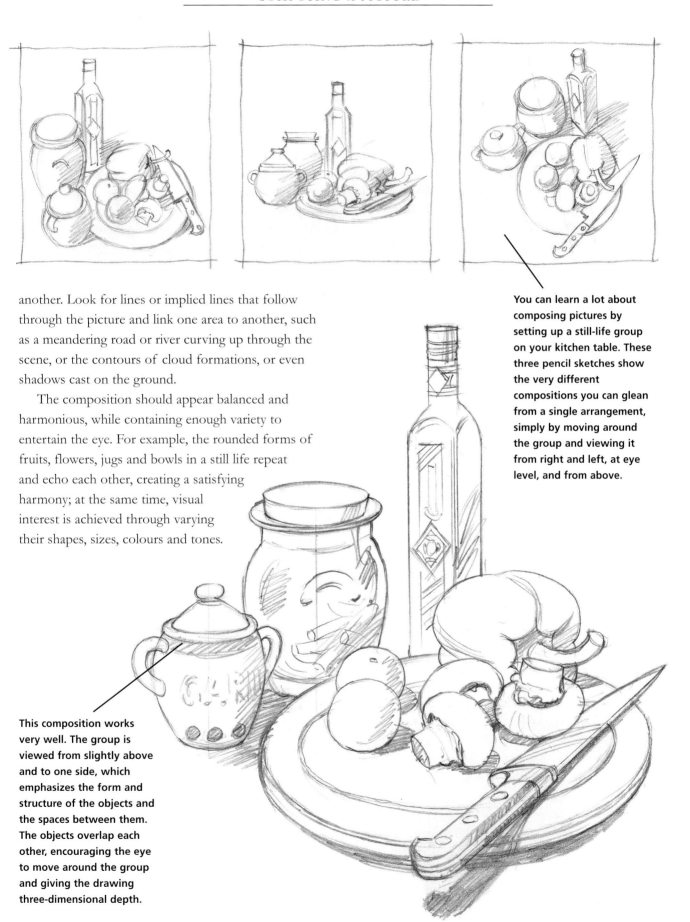

another. Look for lines or implied lines that follow through the picture and link one area to another, such as a meandering road or river curving up through the scene, or the contours of cloud formations, or even shadows cast on the ground.

The composition should appear balanced and harmonious, while containing enough variety to entertain the eye. For example, the rounded forms of fruits, flowers, jugs and bowls in a still life repeat and echo each other, creating a satisfying harmony; at the same time, visual interest is achieved through varying their shapes, sizes, colours and tones.

You can learn a lot about composing pictures by setting up a still-life group on your kitchen table. These three pencil sketches show the very different compositions you can glean from a single arrangement, simply by moving around the group and viewing it from right and left, at eye level, and from above.

This composition works very well. The group is viewed from slightly above and to one side, which emphasizes the form and structure of the objects and the spaces between them. The objects overlap each other, encouraging the eye to move around the group and giving the drawing three-dimensional depth.

Whether you intend to draw a still life for the sheer enjoyment of the shapes, as a study for a painting, or simply as an exercise, you will find that this accessible subject opens up many interesting possibilities and poses many challenges. You may be tempted to draw an existing composition of 'found' objects or to set up your own arrangement.

Still Life and Nature

Nature provides a limitless source of subjects for sketching and drawing. You can study natural subjects outdoors – trees, cloud formations, reflections in water. Or you can gather interesting fragments of nature on country walks – leaves, grasses, pine cones, seashells – and study them at your leisure back at home.

SETTING UP A STILL LIFE

When setting up a still life, don't be tempted to include too much.
A few simple objects, selected for their qualities of shape, form and
texture, will give you plenty to explore and enjoy.

Generally, still life drawings work best when they have a kind of theme, one which has inspired you to draw and which forms the basis of a naturally harmonious picture. For example, you might choose objects which are related through association – flowers and fruits, kitchenware and foodstuffs, plants and gardening implements being some obvious examples.

Or you may be drawn to particular objects purely for their pictorial qualities – shape, colour, tone, texture, pattern – and the contrasts and affinities they display when grouped together.

Composing the group

When you have arranged your still life, move around it and sketch it from different angles and viewpoints to see which makes the better composition. Each change of angle and viewpoint presents fresh possibilities, and you can extend those possibilities even further by using a viewfinder to home in on small sections of the group to create exciting, 'cropped' compositions.

Consider the overall shape of the group you have arranged on the table. Look at it through a viewfinder and decide whether it fits more comfortably within a horizontal or an upright format. Here, for example, a fairly high viewpoint emphasizes the vertical forces within the group and so an upright format is appropriate. The same group drawn in a horizontal format would be surrounded by too much empty space.

This group obviously fits more comfortably into a horizontal format. Try to arrange your still life in a way that emphasizes the form and structure of the objects and the spaces between them. Study how each object relates to the others and be aware of spatial relationships. Small adjustments – moving an apple in front of a vase instead of next to it – will give a sense of depth to the drawing.

There is plenty to think about: does the light cast descriptive shadows that emphasize the form of the objects? Is there a reasonable variety of shapes and tonal contrasts? Examine the relationship not only between the objects themselves but the spaces between them as well; these 'negative' shapes should balance and enhance the 'positive' shapes of the objects, creating a cohesive design.

Choose still-life objects for their shapes, tones and colours, and for the rhythms they create when grouped together. Make sure there is a variety in the shapes and sizes of your objects – tall, short, rounded, angular – and remember that the negative shapes between objects are an important part of the composition. Make quick sketches in which you investigate tonal patterns, shapes, proportions and balance.

A SIMPLE STILL LIFE

Now you are ready to try a simple still life arrangement. Choose a few items from the kitchen – fruit, jugs, pots, a piece of cloth – and arrange them in a composition that pleases you.

For this project you will need a 2B and a 4B pencil, an eraser and a sheet of cartridge paper. Set up your still life group on a table. A piece of fabric draped in folds behind the group will add interest to the background. Make sure there is a variety in the shapes of your objects and try to arrange interesting intervals of space between them. Balance large against small and let some objects overlap others.

Start by lightly sketching in the main outlines of the group and suggesting the background. Check sizes and positions and carefully study how each object relates to the others. Don't complete one object and then move on to the next but try to see the group as a whole and concentrate on getting the overall shapes right.

Modelling the forms

Use shading to define the broad areas of light and shadow on the objects and drapery. Pick out the medium-dark shadows first, depicting them with one or two light layers of hatching. Leave small chinks of white paper to represent the highlights and bright reflections. Then you can develop the gradations of tone that model the forms by adding increasingly darker shading.

Draw a simple 'skeleton' shape of your chosen composition, outlining the basic shapes of the items and how they fit together within the group. Don't worry too much about the finer points of your drawing until you are confident that the main shapes are correct.

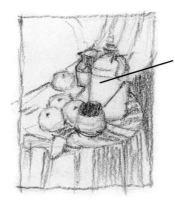

It's a good idea to start by drawing a few quick 'thumbnail' sketches of your proposed arrangement. Try to capture the composition of the whole group in a few simple lines and areas of blocked-in shading. These sketches will help you to decide the viewpoint that works best for your drawing.

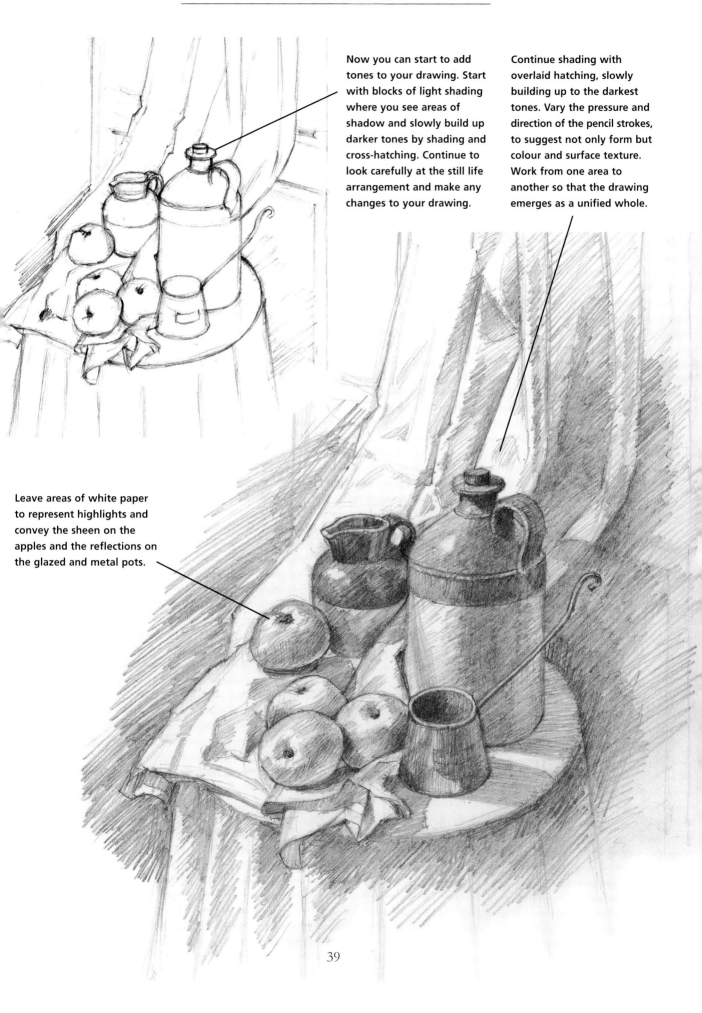

Now you can start to add tones to your drawing. Start with blocks of light shading where you see areas of shadow and slowly build up darker tones by shading and cross-hatching. Continue to look carefully at the still life arrangement and make any changes to your drawing.

Continue shading with overlaid hatching, slowly building up to the darkest tones. Vary the pressure and direction of the pencil strokes, to suggest not only form but colour and surface texture. Work from one area to another so that the drawing emerges as a unified whole.

Leave areas of white paper to represent highlights and convey the sheen on the apples and the reflections on the glazed and metal pots.

DRAWING TEXTURES

The ability to convey texture is vital if you want your drawings to look realistic. Texture provides an opportunity to create decorative interest in a drawing that enlivens the overall composition.

When suggesting a particular texture, consider the full range of marks available to you: short, choppy strokes; nervous, wavy lines; small stippled dots; long curves and loops; even blurs, smears and spots. You can also create an illusion of texture by mirroring the tonal patterns that textures create and by bringing out the ways in which different surfaces reflect light.

Some media and surfaces have inbuilt textural qualities that can be adapted to suit a particular subject. Charcoal dragged on its side across a coarse-grained paper will, for example, produce broken, textured marks that might suggest a rugged cliff face or a gnarled tree trunk. Ink wash on smooth paper lends itself naturally to conveying smooth glass and metal

Use a graphite stick to convey the smooth sheen of a tomato. Apply a light grey tone all over, leaving white highlights. Smooth the tone with a paper stump. Then work over the dark areas again. Draw the stalk with a sharp 2B pencil.

Glass reflects a lot of light, so use mostly pale tones and leave white paper for the sharp, bright highlights. Keep your shading as even as possible to convey the smooth glassy surface.

Capture the hard, knobbly surface of a pineapple with heavy outlines, applying more pressure in the shadow areas. Hatch in each segment, modelling the tiny raised ridges with light and shade.

Crumpled paper forms stiff folds and distinct planes – qualities which you can bring out with hard contour lines and finely hatched shading in the shadow areas, leaving white paper for the sharp highlights.

Lightly sketch in the main outlines of the basket with a 2B pencil. Refer frequently to your subject to check that the shapes and proportions are correct.

Draw the vertical canes, showing how they appear closer together at the curved sides. Start to suggest the plaited wicker, following the curve of the basket.

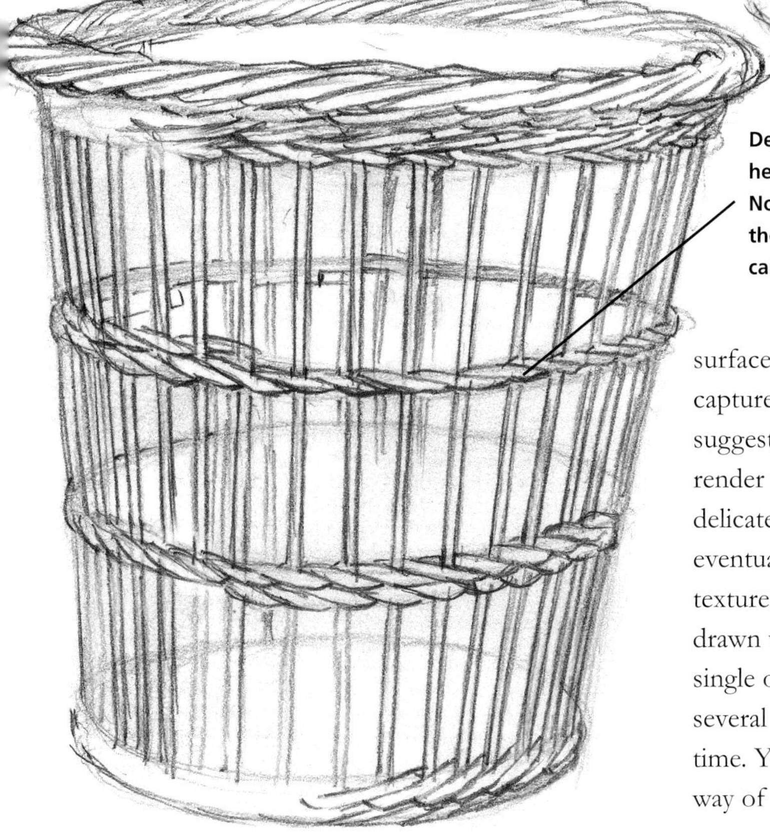

Define the plaited wicker, indicating perspective by using heavier lines at the front and lighter lines at the back. Note also how the individual plaits diminish in size as the basket curves back in space. Shade in the individual canes with finely hatched strokes.

surfaces. The hard angularity of buildings is effectively captured with pen and ink. But these are merely suggestions and there is no reason why you cannot render an animal's soft fur in pen and ink or draw a delicate flower with charcoal. With experience, you will eventually be able to use a single medium to draw any texture: the different textures on these pages were all drawn with simple graphite pencils. Why not take a single object, like the basket shown here, and make several drawings of it using a different medium each time. You will soon discover which ones best suit your way of working.

41

MAKING QUICK SKETCHES

If you are ever stuck for a drawing subject the best advice is just to start drawing – anywhere and anything. Start by sketching simple objects from around your home using pens, pencils and charcoal.

If you are unsure about your ability to draw, the best way to become more confident is to draw constantly. Sketching is a bit like physical exercise: a gentle ten minute walk each day is of more benefit than an exhausting hour of jogging once in a blue moon!

Buy yourself a clutch of sketchbooks – big ones, small ones, spiral-bound and hardback – and keep them everywhere: in your home, your car, your office, your pocket or handbag. Sketchbooks are the perfect place in which to note and record anything that catches your eye, the moment you see it. Try to get into the habit of looking at everything as a potential subject and, sure enough, you will start to see subjects everywhere. It doesn't matter what tool you use to draw with – it can

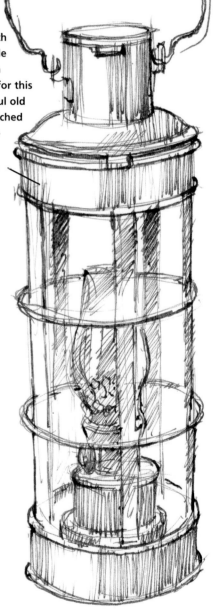

Sepia ink and a dip pen – a medium with a long and venerable history – seemed an appropriate choice for this study of a wonderful old lantern. Vertical hatched strokes describe the reflective surface of the metal casing.

One of the many delights of drawing is discovering the expressive potential of the various drawing media. Here, fluid watercolour washes express the soft and cuddly appeal of a child's teddy bear.

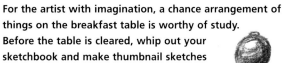

For the artist with imagination, a chance arrangement of things on the breakfast table is worthy of study. Before the table is cleared, whip out your sketchbook and make thumbnail sketches from different viewpoints.

be a pencil, a charcoal stick or even a ballpoint pen. The point is to train your hand to respond to what you see, immediately and instinctively. Every line you draw will add to your experience.

Remember that a drawing doesn't have to be 'perfect' in order to be successful. It doesn't have to be neat and tidy; it doesn't even have to be finished. What matters is that something has awakened your desire to draw and that you have expressed your response to it in a spontaneous and meaningful way.

This coffee mill makes an attractive subject on which to practise drawing cubes and ellipses. The half-opened drawer adds interest to the drawing by breaking up the outline of the square base.

Using coloured pencils sharpened to a fine point, the subtle texture of this Panama hat was created by successive layering of lines in different colours, woven together to create a range of delicate hues.

NATURE STUDIES

*Look around you – the breathtaking variety of shapes, textures,
patterns and colours that can be found in nature offers endless scope
for creative interpretation in sketchbook drawings.*

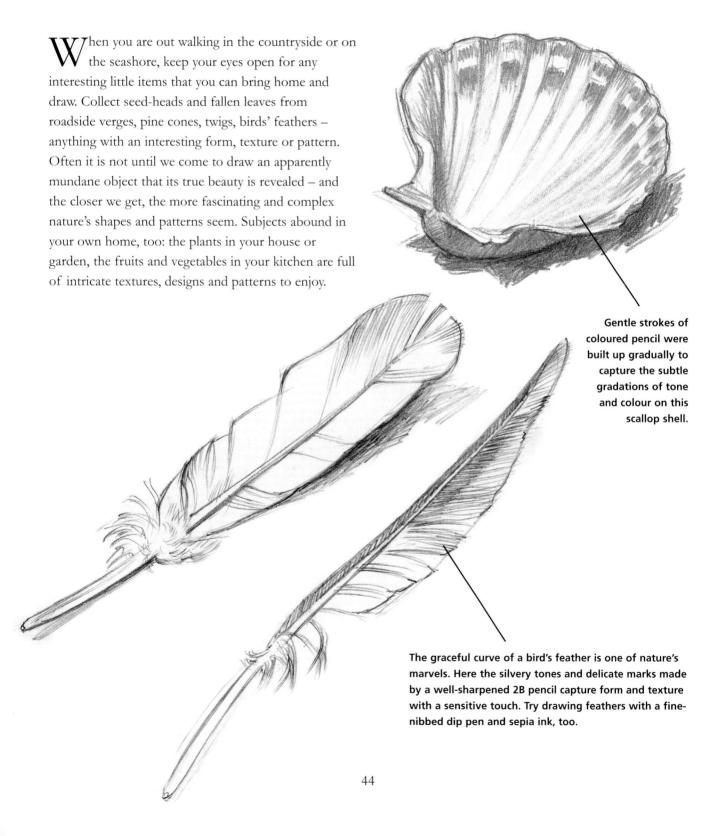

When you are out walking in the countryside or on the seashore, keep your eyes open for any interesting little items that you can bring home and draw. Collect seed-heads and fallen leaves from roadside verges, pine cones, twigs, birds' feathers – anything with an interesting form, texture or pattern. Often it is not until we come to draw an apparently mundane object that its true beauty is revealed – and the closer we get, the more fascinating and complex nature's shapes and patterns seem. Subjects abound in your own home, too: the plants in your house or garden, the fruits and vegetables in your kitchen are full of intricate textures, designs and patterns to enjoy.

Gentle strokes of coloured pencil were built up gradually to capture the subtle gradations of tone and colour on this scallop shell.

The graceful curve of a bird's feather is one of nature's marvels. Here the silvery tones and delicate marks made by a well-sharpened 2B pencil capture form and texture with a sensitive touch. Try drawing feathers with a fine-nibbed dip pen and sepia ink, too.

A closer view of nature's forms can reveal a rich variety of textures and patterns. A mixed-media approach captures every detail of this ivy leaf; an outline in fine-liner pen was filled in with coloured ink, overlaid with marker pen.

The tiny leaf veins were added using gouache paint applied with a very fine brush. Gouache allows you to paint light over dark. A cast shadow drawn with marker pen overlaid with coloured pencil gives the drawing three-dimensionality.

Oil pastels make thick, buttery strokes and are ideal for drawing solid, heavily textured objects like this piece of rock. Try drawing on a textured paper, which breaks up the marks and creates a suitably grainy effect.

The thin, scratchy lines made by a dip pen and ink search out the intricacies of a gnarled old hawthorn branch. As you draw, vary the pressure on the nib so as to create undulating lines which vary from light and thin to heavy and swollen.

It can be absorbing and instructive to interpret the particular qualities of a natural object such as a leaf, a feather, a stone or a twig through the character of the medium you use and the marks you make with it. A sweep of charcoal or pastel over rough paper, for instance, mimics the rough texture of rocks, stones and gnarled wood, while delicate shading with a coloured pencil on smooth paper will convey the silky texture of a flower petal.

A NATURAL STILL LIFE

Willow charcoal is the perfect medium with which to express the
natural spontaneity of this composition of shells, starfish and
driftwood abandoned on the beach by the retreating tide.

The seaside is a treasure trove of fascinating natural objects. Bring home pebbles, shells, starfish, pieces of driftwood and any other bits of flotsam and jetsam you find in order to study and draw them in detail. Even better, make drawings on the spot: when you can feel the sand under your feet and sniff the salt air, you are more attuned to your subject and this will come through in drawings that are fresh and lively.

Using a thin stick of willow charcoal, loosely sketch the main outlines of the objects in the group. Draw lightly so that you can erase any mistakes easily (do this by 'knocking back' the charcoal marks with a putty eraser or a piece of cloth).

Start to define the contrasting textures and patterns of the objects in the group using a variety of lines, strokes and dots. Charcoal is fragile and snaps when applied with pressure; you may find it easier to draw with a short piece of charcoal than with a whole stick.

Look out for objects that have contrasting shapes, textures and tones to make your still life arrangement as varied and interesting as possible.

For this project, find a large sheet of pastel paper and a stick or two of willow charcoal and make a bold, expressive drawing of a 'seaside still life'. If you don't have access to the seaside, try to find some leaves, twigs, pine cones and so on instead. Charcoal is wonderfully expressive. You can snap off a small piece and draw fast, incisive lines with a sharp corner; you can lay the charcoal stick on its side and sweep it over the paper to make broad, grainy marks; and you can blend the powdery marks with your finger to create a range of rich, velvety tones. Charcoal is an excellent medium for beginners because it forces you to draw broadly and not get involved in fiddly details. It is also a forgiving medium, easily erased and overdrawn and ideal for exploratory drawings.

Give form and volume to the pebbles, shells and rock by lightly shading in the shadowed parts and blending the strokes with your fingertip. Use the point of the stick to add more linear details to the driftwood, rock and shells. Spray your finished drawing with fixative to prevent smudging.

FLOWERS AND PLANTS

In order to draw flowers convincingly, you need to understand and be able to draw their basic forms and structures. Why not fill an entire sketchbook with studies of individual flowers and leaves?

Sketching plants and flowers in their natural environment is a pleasant activity but bringing living specimens indoors gives you the opportunity to study their shapes, forms and colours in privacy and peace. Pencil is the ideal medium for observational drawing as it can be erased and corrected with ease. However, colour is one of the most alluring aspects of a flower, so get out your pastels, watercolours, coloured pencils and inks and enjoy yourself!

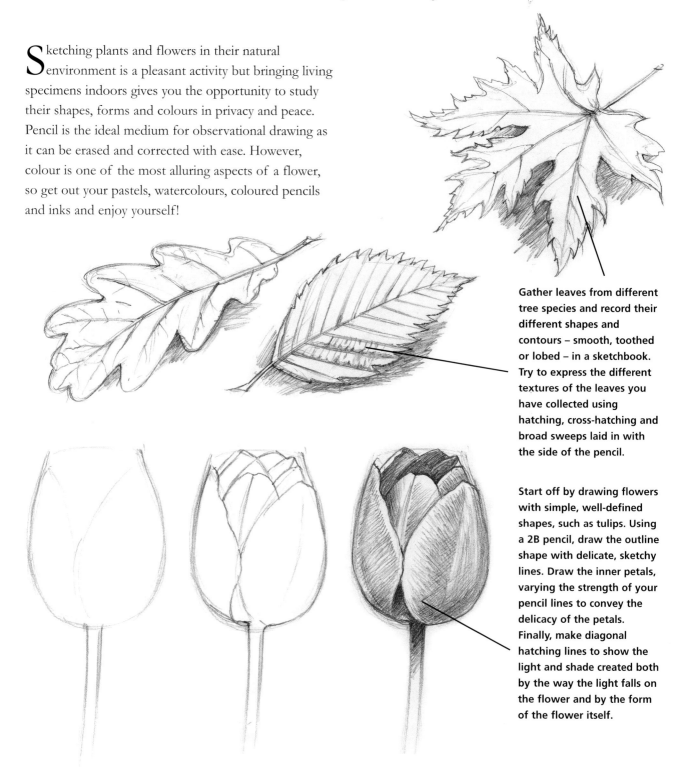

Gather leaves from different tree species and record their different shapes and contours – smooth, toothed or lobed – in a sketchbook. Try to express the different textures of the leaves you have collected using hatching, cross-hatching and broad sweeps laid in with the side of the pencil.

Start off by drawing flowers with simple, well-defined shapes, such as tulips. Using a 2B pencil, draw the outline shape with delicate, sketchy lines. Draw the inner petals, varying the strength of your pencil lines to convey the delicacy of the petals. Finally, make diagonal hatching lines to show the light and shade created both by the way the light falls on the flower and by the form of the flower itself.

The transparency of watercolour is ideal for the fragile forms of flower petals. Note where the lightest lights are and leave these as white paper. Before applying the first delicate wash, gently dampen the area to be painted with a fine brush. Apply increasingly darker tones to the flower while the underlying washes are still damp so that they merge to form subtle, translucent effects; if the paper is dry, the washes will dry leaving a noticeable line.

Try using mixed media to capture the distinctive characteristics of flowers. Here, for example, the lily petals were washed in freely with watercolour and allowed to dry. The delicate striped markings were then picked out using coloured pencils.

Initial observation

Careful observation will help you to understand the subtle and intricate forms of petals, leaves and stems, so make lots of detailed drawings of flowers and plants in close-up. Start by sketching in the main shapes, breaking down the flowers and leaves into simple geometric forms. Daisies, pansies and sunflowers are basically circles and ellipses; tulips and lilies are cups and cones; roses and chrysanthemums are balls and spheres. Let this be your starting point.

When you are happy with the basic outline, you can start to introduce detail and shading. This is the tricky bit because you have to be able to describe shape and form convincingly, while at the same time conveying a sense of the flower as a living, growing, fragile thing. Hold your pencil lightly and draw with sensitive, flowing lines; hard outlines make a flower look hard and wooden. Observe how the leaf stalks join the main stem of the plant and how the petals overlap. Look at the shapes of the spaces between the flowers and stems; this will help you to draw them more accurately.

A VASE OF FLOWERS

Pastels, with their velvety, sumptuous colours, are ideally suited to drawing flowers. Start off with a simple arrangement set against a plain background and practise blending and layering colour.

When arranging flowers for drawing, try to make them appear natural: formal displays of multi-coloured blooms should be avoided in favour of simple arrangements of harmonious colour, perhaps with some foliage to add contrast. Be mindful of creating interesting shapes on your paper and arrange the flowers so that they fan gracefully outwards as well as upwards. Make sure that the blooms are positioned at different heights, face in different directions and that some overlap others.

Try not to get involved in detail straight away: think of your vase of flowers as a single form and establish the broad areas of colour or tone first. You can then build up gradually to the smaller details. Note the size and position of one flower in relation to another and compare the height and spread of the flowers in relation to the vase (a common mistake is to make them look too cramped and small).

Try to avoid drawing outlines and filling them in with colour or tone; use gestural marks to capture the 'personality' of the flower. Pastel is ideal for this approach because you can use its flat side to sweep in areas of 'soft-focus' colour and make expressive strokes that follow the shape of a petal or leaf.

Lightly sketch in the composition with a light grey pastel or pastel pencil. Start with the vase, then rough in the overall shape of the flowers before drawing them individually.

Block in the background with neutral colours, using the pastels on their sides. Fill in the basic colours of the flowers, stems and leaves, blending the pastel strokes with your fingertip.

Work into the flowers with the pastel tips to develop details such as the tiny petals on the daisies. Model the curved petals of the lilies using overlaid strokes of grey-green for the shadowed parts. Suggest light and shade on the leaves using warm and cool greens.

Develop the flower stems, using dark green for the inner ones and various light greens for the outer ones. Don't define them too much – the flowers are the centre of interest. Suggest the colours reflected in the water and the glass vase with grey and white pastels.

There is no doubt that landscape is the most popular subject for drawing and painting. Apart from the wealth of material to inspire you – you can choose anything from a single leaf to a panoramic vista of trees, fields and sky – there is the added delight of being in the countryside 'communing with nature'.

Landscapes and Seascapes

The ever-changing sea is a more challenging prospect for the artist. Waves, foam, breakers and swells require a great deal of patience and experience to capture. But beach scenes and harbour scenes are excellent subjects to start off with. As with landscapes, you can choose to home in on just one element – such as people on the beach, cliffs and dunes, boats and boatyards. Here, the sea becomes part of the scene and is easier to deal with.

SELECTING A VIEW

Walking around the landscape, looking for potential subjects, can be confusing as compositional choices may compete for your attention. A viewfinder is an excellent way of assessing the possibilities.

When confronted with a complex subject like a landscape it can be difficult to decide what to draw. Start by taking a walk round with your sketchbook and a cardboard viewfinder (see page 32), and note down anything that really grabs your attention. From any one position there may be several directions of view that offer subjects to draw, and within each view there may be several aspects that tempt you to explore further.

A viewfinder is extremely useful because it helps to train your eye to see potential subjects and to compose them well. When the scene is concentrated within the window of the frame, you can see at a glance how it will look on paper. Bring the viewfinder closer to your eye to include a wide-angle view; hold it away from you to select a small area. Raise or lower it to alter the position of the horizon line, depending on whether you

With the horizontal (landscape) format the eye can roam from side to side and the mood is one of calm and restfulness.

With the upright (portrait) format the vertical elements become more dominant. The mood becomes more enclosed and intimate.

However you frame your subject, make sure that the focus of interest is placed off-centre. Here the curved path draws the eye to the focal point, which is located at the intersection of thirds.

This sketch conveys a strong sense of space on a small scale by means of both the sharp perspective of the centrally placed road and the set-back position of the focal point.

want to emphasize the sky or the landscape features. Don't just look at your subject horizontally; remember you can turn the viewfinder upright and work with it in a vertical format, too.

You may find that what appeared at first glance to be a good composition reveals unexpected flaws on closer scrutiny, and that simply altering your position slightly improves it dramatically. In fact, by using your viewfinder to isolate various small sections of a scene, you may well discover several interesting compositions to explore, all from the same source.

COMPOSING A LANDSCAPE

No matter how breathtaking a landscape view is, you may find that you have to select and rearrange the elements of the scene in order to create a more balanced image.

Once you have chosen a landscape view, walk around it with your viewfinder and make rapid sketches to see how the composition looks on paper. Try to forget, for the moment, about 'trees, fields and clouds' and think instead of 'lines, shapes and tones'. These elements should be arranged on the paper so that there is one main area of interest, supported by secondary features which lead the eye from the foreground, into and around the picture, eventually coming to rest at the focal point.

Start by breaking the scene down into large, simple areas based on sky, horizon and foreground. Make sure the horizon doesn't cut across the middle of the paper as this creates identical spaces on either side of it, which is boring. Position it in either the upper third of the picture or the lower, depending on whether you want to emphasize the sky or the land. Place the focal point somewhere off-centre, at a point that is a different distance from each edge of the paper, thus creating balance without boredom.

Try to ensure that similar shapes are echoed throughout the picture, knitting the diverse elements

together. At the same time, introduce subtle contrasts that entertain the eye: angular and flowing shapes, busy areas and quiet areas, light and dark tones, bright and muted colours.

These three sketches show how even a slight change of viewpoint can alter the balance of shapes and tones, and even the mood, of the scene. A soft pencil is ideal for making thumbnail sketches because you can get down the features and the tonal areas quickly.

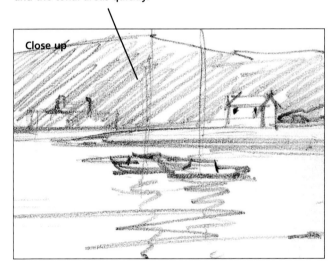

Close up

Mid-distance

Far away

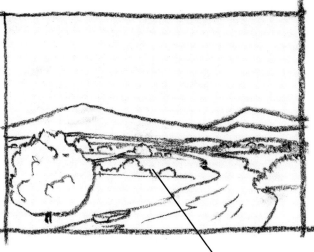

For a simple landscape, an uneven division of land and sky is usually preferable to a mid-page horizon. By making the foreground the largest area you can add to the illusion of space and depth. Opt for a low horizon if you want to emphasize a dramatic skyline.

Natural features of the landscape often provide strong cues for the arrangement of a composition. In this sketch, the curve of the country lane sweeps down from the foreground, leading the eye into the middle distance, where it is then led upward in a criss-cross fashion by the linear patterns of fields and hedgerows to the distant hills.

SKETCHBOOK STUDIES

All the great artists keep copious notes and sketches as reference material for their work, and you should use your own sketchbook to build up a personal record of visual ideas and information.

It is a good idea to buy a small sketchbook – one that fits into your pocket or a bag that you always carry – and to use it whenever the opportunity arises. Try to do a sketch a day, jotting down anything of interest on your travels: street furniture, architectural details, trees, children playing in the park. Sketching regularly will increase your manual dexterity, improve your hand-eye co-ordination and increase your powers of observation. It is only by looking and by becoming familiar with the small details of the subject that you can achieve the confidence which enables you to create drawings with real conviction.

Your sketchbook serves many purposes. It can be a personal visual diary, full of sketches done on location for pure enjoyment that will conjure up pleasant memories of people and places. It can be the seedbed

Several quick sketches, even unfinished ones, can be as valuable as a single, involved study. They solidify your understanding of the overall structure and shapes of your chosen subject.

Armed with a sketch pad and a soft pencil, you can make detailed studies of any interesting buildings or architectural features that you spot. These can later be included in a finished drawing or painting.

The transparency of watercolour is ideally suited to sketching soft clouds and misty skies. Individual cloud studies can be beautiful things in their own right and will provide you with invaluable reference for paintings.

Strong sunlight against threatening sky

Slate roof patches of moss

Dark patches (Damp)

Foreground mainly Ochre

of ideas for finished paintings and drawings. It can be the testing ground for media and techniques you haven't tried before. And it is a reservoir of closely observed details to which you can return again and again: the shapes of clouds, the forms of leaves and flowers, the gesture of a figure.

Sketching materials

Pencil is the most convenient medium for quick sketching, and you can now buy water-soluble pencils: simply moisten a finger and smudge areas where you want to add tone and shadow. Pen and ink creates sinuous, flowing lines as well as tonal washes, and felt-tipped pens and even humble ballpoints have expressive potential. Coloured pencils and watercolour pencils are easy to carry and enable you to record colour quickly and accurately. If you want to try paints, watercolour, acrylic and gouache are handy as they dry quickly.

When making sketches for finished paintings, back up your drawing with written notes that help to describe specific colours and details, the time of day, the weather and light conditions.

Soft pastel is excellent both for quick impressions and highly finished drawings. With a wide range of delicate tints and shades, it is particularly suitable for landscapes and skies.

TONE IN LANDSCAPES

Variations in tone – the lightness or darkness of a subject – will make your drawings clearer, enhance the illusion of depth, and strengthen the composition.

Try to get an active and interesting distribution of light and dark tones throughout your drawing. The overall pattern of lights and darks is important because it forms the skeleton, or framework, that holds the picture together, gives it balance and strength, and makes it easy to 'read'.

Think of the lights and darks in your subject as 'weights' to be balanced and counterbalanced until an equilibrium is found. For example, a large area of light tone on one side of the picture can be balanced by a small area of dark tone on the other side because the dark tone has more visual weight.

Conveying depth

The illusion of space and distance in a landscape can be created solely through variation in tone. Lighter

Hold your pencil in different ways to get different tonal effects. Hold it in the normal 'writing' position for making darker tones and fine detail.

For shading soft tones, hold the pencil lightly between thumb and forefinger with the shaft of the pencil lying under the palm. This will allow for much greater freedom of movement.

Make a tonal drawing of your proposed subject in charcoal or soft pencil, breaking it down into broad tonal areas – light (white), mid-tone (grey) and dark (black). The white paper will be the lightest tone; black can be achieved by adding more pressure on the pencil.

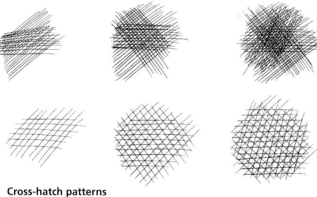

Cross-hatch patterns

Explore different ways of creating tones through marks and lines. The brooding atmosphere of this industrial landscape is captured using a dip pen and Indian ink. The dense and varied tonal areas are built up with a complex network of patiently cross-hatched lines.

The main centre of interest can be stressed dramatically by putting the darkest dark in the picture against the lightest light. Here the white house is accentuated by the dark tones of the trees surrounding it. This area of strong tonal contrast captures and holds the viewer's attention.

tones seem to recede into the distance, while darker ones appear to advance. If you want to create a strong illusion of depth in your landscapes, make the closer elements stronger in tone and the farther things lighter.

If you have difficulty in distinguishing the tones in the scene you are drawing, try squinting at it through half-closed eyes – or don a pair of sunglasses. Either of these will cancel out most of the colour and reduce everything to mere degrees of light and dark.

TREES AND FOLIAGE

Trees make a fascinating study in themselves. Draw them all year round and observe their shapes and growth patterns, from the skeletal winter outline to the abundant masses of summer foliage.

In landscapes, trees are usually seen from a distance, so it is more important to capture their overall shape than to try to draw every leaf and twig. In fact, too much attention to detail can render a tree lifeless. Look first for the overall shape of the tree – is it squat and broad or tall and narrow? Sketch in a rough outline, then look for the broad shapes made by clumps of foliage. Pastel, charcoal and graphite sticks are good media to use for a bold approach.

It's important to get the proportions right: a common mistake is to make the tree canopy too small, resulting in the 'lollipop' effect. Hold your pencil in

Try to define the silhouette and 'gesture' of various tree species and compare their differences. Draw simple tonal sketches like these using a soft medium such as graphite stick. This cherry laurel, for instance, has a squat, rounded silhouette.

The lime tree has a tall, slender silhouette. The foliage masses are long and loose and their direction of growth tends to be downward rather than outward.

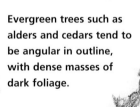

Evergreen trees such as alders and cedars tend to be angular in outline, with dense masses of dark foliage.

Here a quick pencil sketch has been enhanced with simple watercolour washes to create a lively impression of an oak tree in all its summer glory. Notice that the foliage is not a solid mass: there are lots of 'sky holes', particularly around the outer edges of the tree. Paint the sunlit foliage first, with light, warm greens. While the paint is still just damp, apply successive layers of cool, dark, bluish greens for the foliage in shadow.

front of the tree and use it as a measuring tool, comparing the width of the canopy with its height from base to crown. Then compare the proportion of the visible trunk to the overall height of the tree.

Observe and record the way light falls on the tree, defining the volume of trunks, branches and clumps of foliage. Note also how some of the branches grow almost horizontally, while others are almost vertical, and indicate branches that grow towards and away from you as well as sideways. All of this will help to convey form and solidity.

63

LANDSCAPE IN PENCIL

The ordinary graphite pencil has a freshness and immediacy that makes it ideal for outdoor sketching. It is very versatile, capable of suggesting light and atmosphere, space, depth and colour.

Graphite pencils come in a range of grades from hard to soft, and it's important to choose the right grade for the subject and for your style of drawing. An H pencil, for example, has a hard lead and gives only a pale line, no matter how hard you press; a soft pencil such as a 6B can be controlled by pressure to give lines of varying weight and thickness, as well as a wide range of tones from light to dark.

This versatility makes soft pencils an excellent medium for drawing landscapes on the spot. They are speedy and easy to work with, helping you to capture a scene quickly and with minimum fuss – essential when you are working outdoors in changeable conditions.

If you have access to the countryside, why not find a scene that appeals to you and spend a few hours

drawing it with just a couple of pencils – say, a 2B and an 8B. A view like this one, with hills, fields and woodland stretching to the horizon, presents a particular challenge; without the benefit of colour you have to rely on lines and tones alone to create a sense of spatial recession.

Start by sketching in the main outlines of the natural features in the landscape, working lightly so that you can rub out any mistakes easily. Don't start to shade until you are satisfied with the composition. When you start to shade, don't just work up any one area until it's finished: instead, build up the drawing as a whole, moving freely all over the paper. This allows you to check the overall tonal progression from the foreground to the horizon.

Using a 2B pencil, start by plotting the position of the horizon line. Then lightly sketch in the curve of the river, which establishes the perspective of the scene. Briefly outline the important contours of the hills, fields and trees, remembering to make them smaller as the scene recedes towards the horizon. The whole effect should remain free and sketchy at this stage.

You can now start to build up tone and detail. Use a softer, 8B pencil to work gently over the darker parts of the scene with hatched lines. Vary the pressure on the pencil to create a variety of tones, and alter the direction of the strokes to capture the natural features.

Continue to develop the various tones and textures in the scene: use long, evenly spaced hatching for the smooth fields and short lines and scribbles for the trees. Suggest spatial recession using a progression from strong to light tones and a diminishing scale of textural marks into the distance.

LANDSCAPE IN PEN AND INK

In this drawing, the low horizon means that the sky occupies much of the picture area. On to this the strong, dark, sculptural forms of the trees project, linking the earth with the sky.

Some people might regard pen and ink as a rather inflexible medium for drawing landscapes but, as this picture demonstrates, it is in fact capable of producing a wide range of sensitive marks. This drawing was made with a traditional dip pen, which is light, flexible and responsive and produces lively, expressive lines. The pliable nib of a dip pen enables you to make strokes of varying widths and is an excellent medium for freehand drawing.

It is important to note that pen and ink is basically a linear medium: tones are created with hatched and

Working on a sheet of smooth cartridge paper, start by drawing the scene with a sharp HB pencil. Lightly draw the horizon line, positioning it near the bottom of the paper. Then sketch in the outlines of the tree trunks, the main branches and the clumps of foliage, which fill most of the picture area. Finally, put in the road, the houses and the distant trees.

This detail of the finished drawing shows how loose hatching is used to develop tone and texture.

scribbled strokes rather than blending. Once you understand the characteristics of the medium you will soon learn to recognize which subjects lend themselves to its descriptive qualities. This group of trees, for example, is a perfect subject for a pen-and-ink rendering as it has a strong linear emphasis and dense tones and textures.

Creating depth

When deciding on a viewpoint for your landscape drawing, look for elements that will emphasize the feeling of space and depth. In this drawing, the dramatic contrast in scale between the tall foreground trees and the tiny trees and buildings in the background gives a strong impression of space and perspective and at the same time creates a visually arresting composition. The curve of the road sweeps the eye into the distance, further enhancing the experience of three-dimensional space.

Using a dip pen and black ink, start to add tonal detail to the drawing using closely spaced hatched lines. Start with the distant trees, then work on the foreground foliage. Suggest the foreground grasses with zigzag strokes.

Develop the foreground trees, suggesting the texture of the foliage with short, angled strokes. Overlay a further network of hatching for the areas in deepest shadow. Add the shadows on the tree trunks and the cast shadow on the road.

LANDSCAPE IN COLOURED PENCIL

Light, portable and easy to handle, coloured pencils are an excellent medium for rapid drawings and outdoor sketches. They are capable of creating highly detailed effects and rich blends of colour.

Coloured pencils can be used on any paper that has a slight tooth, ranging from cartridge paper to brown wrapping paper. You can achieve effects ranging from pale and delicate to rich and complex: with light pressure on the pencil the colour catches only on the 'peaks' of the paper surface, producing a subtle, grainy effect. With heavier pressure the colour is pushed into the 'troughs' of the paper. The paper surface is slightly flattened and the pigment spreads to create a smooth, fluid layer.

Creating colour

There are many different ways of 'mixing' colours on the paper surface. By using the hatching technique of laying a series of roughly parallel lines in different colours or tones you will achieve an optical mixing effect which is far richer and more vibrant than a flat

area of colour. For example, strokes of blue laid over yellow make a green that is more subtle and lively than the flat colour you get by using a single green pencil. The pure yellow and blue are discernible but from a distance they merge and 'read' as green. You can also lay one set of hatched lines over another in a different direction to create complex colour effects – a technique called cross-hatching.

Alternatively, you can create smooth tones and colours by using the side of the pencil lead to lay down thin layers of colour, one over the other. Don't press too hard: stroke lightly so that you build up thin veils of colour that allow those beneath to remain visible. Because the coloured pigment is semi-transparent, light reflects off the white paper and up through the colours, lending them a soft luminosity similar to that produced by watercolour paints.

For this project, choose a sheet of slightly textured white drawing paper. This will become part of the finished picture, showing through the pencil marks and creating bright areas of cloud and crisp highlights. Start by sketching in the main elements of the composition with a neutral-coloured pencil such as grey or blue. Fill in the sky area with loosely hatched diagonal strokes of pale blue pencil, leaving patches of bare paper for the clouds.

Lightly hatch over the hills and trees with directional strokes of yellow and pale green. Fill in the patch of water with strokes of turquoise and the distant corn field with orange. Define the curve of the road and the shape of the bridge with tones of grey. Darken the distant hills with strokes of blue, letting the pale greens show through.

Develop the landscape features in more detail, hatching and cross-hatching using different colours and directional strokes to create colour and tone. Work over the distant hills with loose strokes of purple.

LANDSCAPE IN WATERCOLOUR

In this project traditional watercolour techniques are used to depict an idyllic landscape with bright cumulus clouds above corn fields and trees bathed in the warm light of a September afternoon.

Watercolour is a marvellous medium for sketching landscapes because of its speed, freshness and ability to capture the fleeting effects of light and atmosphere. Ideally, landscapes should be painted on location rather than from photographs: a picture painted directly from nature has a freshness and immediacy that cannot be reproduced in the studio.

A working method

Although watercolour is a spontaneous medium, you have to work methodically in order to keep your work fresh and lively; too much fiddling and prodding will result in muddy, overworked washes. Take the time to plan the sequence of washes you are going to use and apply them quickly and decisively. Always work from light to dark: start by laying in pale tones in thin, broad washes and work up to the dark tones with successive

applications of thin layers of colour. Establish the large colour masses first, working broadly with the largest brush you can. Leave the detailed refinements till last, added with a smaller brush if necessary.

A limited palette

Working with a limited range of colours is not only practical for outdoor work – the less equipment you have to carry, the better – it is also better for your painting as you will be more likely to achieve a harmonious colour balance. A variety of landscape greens, for instance, can be created mixing together just one yellow and one blue; by using more blue in the mix you make darker, cooler greens, and by using more yellow you make lighter, warmer greens. And because the same colours are repeated throughout, it helps to tie the image together and give it a satisfying unity.

For this project you will need a piece of Not surface watercolour paper taped to a board; a medium-size, round brush; a handful of colours such as French ultramarine and lemon yellow (for the greens) and raw sienna (for the clouds and corn field); a mixing palette and a jar of water. Sketch out the composition very lightly with an HB pencil. It is best not to draw the outlines of the clouds as you want them to be soft, loose shapes. Then dampen the paper with clean water.

Start by painting the sky, leaving ragged shapes for the clouds. Paint the undersides of the clouds with raw sienna. Note the perspective of the clouds, which appear darker, smaller and closer together as they near the horizon. Then block in the corn field, trees and haystacks.

Let the painting dry and then apply layers of stronger colour, gradually building up the forms with thin overlays. Use darker tones of green to model the forms of the trees and haystacks with shadow. Use the tip of the brush to add the finer details.

WATERSCAPE IN PENCIL

This simple pencil drawing captures the stillness and quality of light of late afternoon. The smooth, still surface of the canal faithfully mirrors the buildings, while a few small ripples break the symmetry.

There is something pictorially satisfying about a smooth body of water reflecting the landscape lining its banks. Trees, buildings and bridges, and their soft reflections in the water, present a balanced and unified image that is pleasing to the eye. The only problem is that water is constantly on the move. This is where a camera comes in useful – a photograph freezes the action and allows you to study the shapes of waves, ripples and reflections in a given instant. Once you have gained confidence by drawing from photographs, you will be able to work directly from the subject, which is always preferable.

Achieving the fluid, reflective appearance of water requires surprisingly little effort. Omit all superfluous details and put in only the major shapes and reflections, drawing them with rapid, calligraphic strokes. The more simply water is depicted, the wetter it looks!

Perspective problems

A common problem for beginners is that of making a body of water 'lie down' on a horizontal plane as it recedes into the distance. If the perspective is wrong, the water may appear to be sloping uphill! Make sure that the stream or river in your drawing becomes narrower as it recedes into the distance.

Another point to watch out for is the perspective of waves and ripples; as they recede into the distance they appear smaller, flatter and more closely spaced. Pay attention to reflections, too – unlike shadows, they don't come forward but appear to go straight down into the water.

Drawing bends in a river also presents problems of perspective. As the river curves out of view, its shape becomes very much narrower; if the angle of the bend is drawn too wide, the river appears to slope upwards.

A quick thumbnail sketch will help you to decide where to position the horizon line and the focal point of the scene, as well as the tonal arrangement.

Use a soft pencil to make an outline sketch of the scene, including the major reflections and highlights on the water. Carefully check the perspective of the canal.

The atmosphere of this drawing stems from the placement of simple shapes of dark tone contrasted with the broad areas of bright sky and water. Use the side of the pencil lead to shade in all the dark areas with a single grey tone.

The focal point is the dark building and its reflection, so stress these by making them the areas of darkest tone. Press harder with the pencil now, building up layers of dense hatching. Finally, work into the highlights on the water and pick out details and textures along the canal banks.

SKETCHING AT THE BEACH

The seaside is a favourite haunt of artists because it presents a limitless supply of imagery. Sea, sky and sand provide an ever-changing backdrop for the hustle and bustle of human activity.

Nowhere in Britain is very far from the sea and our coastline is incredibly varied, ranging from dramatic steep cliffs and wild marshy estuaries with huge skies, to picturesque fishing villages, sandy coves and bays, and jolly seaside resorts. There are so many different aspects to explore and your sketches can incorporate everything from the intricate pattern on a tiny seashell to the vast spaces of sea and sky, which change from hour to hour, minute to minute according to the weather and the time of day.

Make quick sketches that capture the essence of the scene, and more studied drawings of details that interest you – a piece of driftwood, an old lobster pot, a colourful windbreak, the reflections in a rock pool. Before long you will have built up a wealth of reference material which you can use in future drawings and paintings and you will have passed a very pleasant day increasing your skills of drawing and observation!

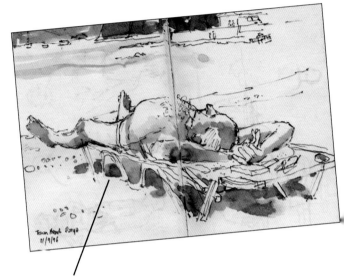

This ink line-and-wash sketch, drawn right across two pages of a sketchbook, is an amusing character study as well as a marvellous evocation of summer heat.

In this drawing a soft pencil was used on its side to capture the drama of white surf crashing on the rocks, accentuated by the dark tone of the sky behind.

The beach is a great place to draw foreshortened figures. A felt-tipped pen encourages a fast, linear approach.

When the crowds have gone home at the end of the day, the beach takes on a completely different aspect. This sensitive watercolour study was painted on a pre-stretched watercolour pad. Note how the dark, solid shapes of the groynes accentuate the luminosity of the sky and water.

Boats are tricky subjects to draw – they curve from front to back and the hulls bulge from top to bottom. It is best to concentrate on the proportions first. Constantly look at your subject as you draw, analyzing shapes and comparing angles.

Wonderful figure compositions occur on beaches, where families and friends relax together and adopt unstudied poses that have a natural grace. Whether sunbathing, gazing out to sea or reading, the figures remain inert for long periods, allowing you to sketch them at your leisure. With a small sketchbook you can mingle with the holidaymakers and be unobtrusive and unnoticed while you sketch. If there is strong sun, try to find a shady spot in which to work or take a sun umbrella. Shade is essential for your drawings as well as for you as the glare of bright sunlight on white paper makes colours and tones difficult to assess.

A very quick study using pen and waterproof ink overlaid with watercolour washes. Accents of white paper convey the effect of bright sunlight, which produces strong highlights on the water's surface and on the heads, shoulders and forearms of the figures.

HARBOUR IN COLOURED PENCIL

There is a special quality of light and colour about harbours and the sea. To capture the intense Mediterranean light in this scene, vibrant blues are played against warm earths and sparkling touches of white.

Small fishing harbours, creeks, bays, inlets and coves provide an endless source of material for drawings and sketches. Coloured pencils are ideal for drawing colourful subjects like the one in this project because they combine the speed and linear quality of graphite pencils with the added bonus of colour. Just one word of warning: a set of coloured pencils looks very appealing and the temptation is to use every single one in your drawing! You must resist that temptation and keep to a fairly limited range of colours so that your picture has an overall harmony. In this drawing, blues and greens predominate, and the colourful houses and boats are suggested with contrasting touches of orange. Most of the tonal values are light and touches of white paper are left bare, all of which helps to create an impression of colour and shimmering light.

Composing the picture

With marine subjects there is so much material it is hard to know where to begin. As well as sky and water there is all the bustling activity of quays, wharves, piers and jetties, and of course boats, with their jumble of masts, sails and rigging. And harbours are just as interesting when the tide is out: there are winding channels, pools and reflections on the muddy bottom, boats tilted at crazy angles, and an assortment of mooring ropes, buoys and flotsam and jetsam left by the receding waters. Walk around the harbour with your sketchbook and viewfinder and choose an aspect of the scene that will make for an interesting composition. In the project drawing, for instance, there is a nice balance between the busy shapes of the boats, houses and trees and the quiet passages of sky and water.

Working on a sheet of cartridge paper with a slight tooth, start by sketching out the composition lightly with a soft pencil. Draw the major shapes first – the water and rocks in the lower part of the picture and the overlapping hills and trees in the upper part. Then draw in the boats.

Shade in the sky, the warm greens of the trees and hill, and the earth colour of the far bank and its reflection. Use horizontal strokes for the water, leaving white shapes for the boats and their reflections.

Deepen the blue of the upper sky to bring it forward. Model the forms of the hill and trees with darker greens. Jot in the roofs and windows of the houses with pale tones to keep them in the distance. Model the foreground rocks with line and shading. Deepen the tone of the water and suggest ripples on the surface with short strokes.

Most of us nowadays live in towns and cities where buildings and street scenes offer a readily accessible subject for sketching and drawing. Walk down your local street and you will find a wealth of shapes, patterns and textures that provide the raw material for exciting pictures. There are many aspects to explore in the urban environment, from closely observed details of individual buildings to entire streets bustling with people and cars.

Buildings and Streets

Whatever aspect of urban life you decide to draw, try to choose a medium and a technique that expresses it to the full. You might choose a linear medium such as pen and ink to record the intricate details of a carved statue; if you want to express the colour and bustle of a street market you might try a bold drawing in oil pastels; or you might decide that ink line-and-wash is the perfect medium with which to capture the play of light and shadow on sunlit buildings. There are no rules – so experiment.

RECORDING DETAILS

As well as overall drawings of buildings, make sketches and studies of specific details, patterns and textures which you can use as reference for a more considered drawing or painting back home.

Buildings are often rich with details that give them individual character and make them fascinating subjects to draw. With older buildings, in particular, features such as doors, windows, arches, balconies and architectural mouldings can make intriguing subjects in themselves. When you are walking around city streets, keep a sketchbook handy so you can jot down anything of interest. A simple pen or pencil will describe the delicate tracery of wrought-iron gates and balconies with calligraphic lines; use pastel, oil pastel or marker pens to jot in colourful verandas and shop awnings that create lively patterns within the overall framework of a shopping street.

When it comes to drawing street scenes, it isn't necessary to define every window, brick and roof tile – a small area of texture can imply the whole. Broken lines, dots and dashes will give an impression of intricate detail, while gentle watercolour tints convey volume and solidity and the play of light and shadow.

Careful study of the shadows creates solidity and monumentality in this small pencil sketch of an old stone doorway. Notice the gradation of the shadow inside the arch. Hold the pencil on its side for broad shading and use the point for picking out linear details.

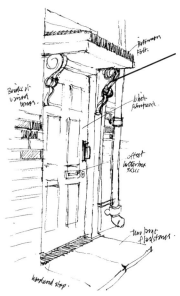

Pen and ink is a medium which is very effective in recording buildings and architectural details. As well as an overall sketch of the subject, you can make written notes about colours, tones and intricate details.

Don't be too precise when drawing windows. Here, the edges of the colour washes don't follow the lines of the glazing bars exactly, and most of the glass panes are left unpainted, helping to integrate the window into its surroundings.

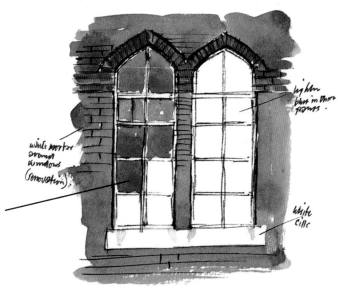

With experience you will develop a kind of visual shorthand that suggests rather than labours over the details of buildings.

Suggesting texture

When drawing textural elements such as brickwork, stone, stucco or wood, first study the texture carefully and then consider how you might explore the potential of your materials for interpreting these surfaces. If you are using pencil or coloured pencil, different types of line and tonal shading using the pencil on its side will describe the overall 'feel' of the building material, while jagged lines drawn with a sharpened tip will suggest linear details such as cracks in stonework or peeling plasterwork. A textured paper is often useful: when charcoal or pastel is laid on its side and lightly dragged across the surface a textured mark results which can suggest pitted stone or weathered brick. Smooth surfaces such as glass and marble can be described by blending with fingers or a torchon, and highlights can be 'lifted out' of a dark tonal area with an eraser.

When a building is viewed from ground level, vertical perspective comes into play. Use your pencil to check the angles of the receding lines of roofs and chimney stacks.

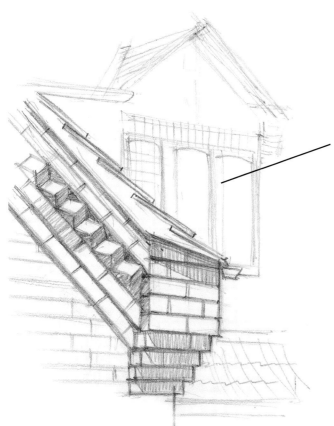

Many subjects suitable for detailed pencil work can be found on buildings. Here, a 3B pencil records the intricate arrangement of bricks and tiles on the corner of a house.

When you are drawing a building you should avoid over-defining details and textures. However, it is worth making close-up studies of walls and roofs in order to understand their structure and develop a technique to record it. Coloured pencils were used to draw these terracotta roof tiles.

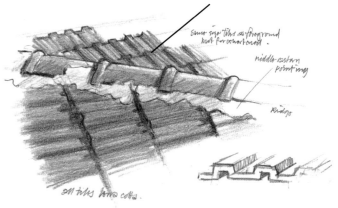

A BUILDING IN WATERCOLOUR

*This beautiful country house with a grand curved drive sweeping up
to the front door cries out to have its 'portrait' painted. So get out
your watercolour paints and have a go!*

No matter how grand and imposing a building might be, its construction is still basically that of a cube, or a series of cubes. If you can draw a box in perspective, you can draw a building in perspective, and once you've got that right, the rest – doors, windows, chimneys, balconies – is just icing on the cake. So start with a well-constructed drawing and check all the angles and proportions before you start to add colour.

Choosing a viewpoint

When a house is the main focus of interest in a picture it's important to show it to advantage and bring out its individual character. Walk around the site and find the best, most flattering angle of view. Decide whether you want to move in close, or include some of the surrounding scenery. The light is important, too, as

shadows can help to explain forms and accentuate details and textures. As a rule it is best to avoid painting or drawing in the middle of the day, when the sun is high in the sky and casts minimal shadows. Most artists prefer early morning or late afternoon, when the sun casts long, descriptive shadows.

This house is viewed at a 45 degree angle, so two-point perspective comes into play (see pages 26-27). Two of its walls are visible, so there are two sets of perspective lines converging towards two vanishing points on the horizon line. Obviously it would be easier to draw the house from a straightforward frontal view – no perspective problems to deal with – but as you can see from this picture, an oblique viewpoint enhances the scale and grandeur of the building and stresses its three-dimensional volume and solidity.

Make a careful drawing of the house with a well-sharpened pencil. Start by lightly indicating the horizon line. Draw the vertical line at the front edge of the house. Draw the angles of the receding planes of the roof and extend these to the horizon line to fix the vanishing points on either side of the house. It is now a relatively simple task to complete the overall shape of the building and to establish the angles of the doors and windows. Then you can lightly indicate the landscape setting.

Paint the sky and trees in the background and leave to dry before painting the local colours of the house. Then put in the foreground grass and flowers and the foliage along the front of the house. Allow the painting to dry.

Suggest the window panes with tiny squares of medium and dark tone, leaving thin slivers of white paper for the glazing bars. Apply transparent dark washes over the shadow end of the house, under the eaves and beneath the window sills. Suggest the pattern of the brickwork and add more detail to the foliage.

DIFFERENT TYPES OF BUILDINGS

From your local town to an exotic holiday location, from farmyard to urban wasteland, man-made structures of all types are a continual source of inspiration and provide opportunities for creative drawing.

Making a detailed study of an individual building has a twofold reward: drawing skills are extended by exploring perspective, shape, form and tone, and a greater appreciation of the building itself is developed through the close observation required to draw it.

Whether in the town or the country, you are sure to come across an interesting building that inspires you to draw. There is no need to restrict yourself to drawing grand cathedrals, imposing mansions and picturesque cottages: ramshackle old buildings often have more potential than conventionally 'pretty' ones. Wrecks and ruins are fascinating subjects for creative interpretation because they have weathered and changed shape as parts of the original structure have fallen away, paint has peeled and stone has cracked. Modern buildings, too, make exciting subjects for pictures, with their bold geometric lines, shimmering glass facades and sky-scraping steel columns. With the industrial heritage of many cities, there are factories, petro-chemical plants, wharves, chimneys and cranes – not the most attractive structures, but you can make dramatic, moody tonal drawings of them in charcoal or black ink and wash.

Choose your medium to suit the subject: a delicate line-and-wash drawing will capture the play of light and shadow on an ornate facade, while pastel and charcoal convey the pitted surface of weathered stone.

Even in a simple pencil sketch, try to relate the building you are drawing to its surroundings. Here, vigorous hatching helps to tie together the windmill and the sky.

The variety of line and mark that is possible with a dip pen is ideal for this type of detailed drawing. Texture and shading are suggested here with line alone.

Many old buildings look as if they have grown naturally out of the landscape they sit in. Try to achieve a similar harmony in your sketches, using the same loose techniques for the building as for the landscape.

Ruined old farm buildings are often so well integrated into the landscape that they almost appear to be organic forms, like the surrounding hills and trees. In this watercolour study there is a harmonious interplay of textures: crumbling bricks, rusting corrugated iron and overgrown brambles.

A STREET SCENE IN PASTEL

Coloured pastels allow you to produce 'painted' drawings on the spot with a minimum of fuss. The results combine the airy sketchiness of a drawing with the rich colour values of a painting.

The sharp contrast of sunlight and shadow in a narrow back street makes this an attractive subject for a pastel drawing. The shadow tones create a natural frame for the figures, which act as colourful 'punctuation marks' leading the eye down the street towards the sunlit white building in the distance.

Sketching in public spaces may seem daunting but drawing on the spot forces you to work quickly and make instant decisions, which results in lively drawings. One hazard that's hard to avoid is the curious onlooker: a useful tip is to sit with your back to a wall, so that at least no one can peer over your shoulder.

Take your sketchbook and a camera and collect plenty of reference material to be able to work up a finished drawing or painting back at home.

Working in pastel

Pastels are ideal for the travelling artist as they are light, easy to carry and the equipment required is minimal. Working in pastel combines both drawing and painting skills. You can treat it as a linear medium for outlines and loosely hatched textures, or the colour may be laid in broad, grainy patches and blended with the fingers or a rag. It is important to keep the surface of the picture light and open in the early stages, to avoid clogging the grain of the paper with pigment and making the surface unworkable. Pastel colour is soft and powdery and liable to smudging, so it is advisable to spray the finished drawing with fixative.

Sketch out the composition with charcoal. Draw lightly, keeping the lines loose and sketchy so that you can easily brush them off if you need to make alterations.

Build up the shadow tones with blended strokes. Using the tips and sharp corners of the sticks, draw the windows, doors and balconies with dark pastels. Finally, add definition to the figures.

Snap off short lengths of pastel and, laying the pieces on their sides, apply broad strokes of grainy colour to lay in the main shapes and colour masses. Smooth the strokes on the broad areas by lightly rubbing with your fingers. Work carefully around the white shapes on the figures and the distant building. Start to add spots of colour to the figures.

STREET LIFE

Try to capture something of the restless energy of the city in your
street scenes – the ebb and flow of people going about their business,
the hubbub of traffic, the colour and noise.

Jostling crowds may be annoying and motor cars noisy and smelly, but they are a part of urban life and should be included in your street scenes – unless you are drawing a ghost town! If the prospect seems daunting, remember that you are aiming for a quick impression and faithful accuracy is not what is required.

The human element

As well as giving the image a sense of scale, figures add life and movement which contrasts with the fixed solidity of the surrounding buildings. Simplify figures

to the bare essentials, especially if they are in the distance. Capture the overall shape and gesture by looking at the angles of head, hips and limbs, then flesh out the figures into simple silhouettes. Hands, feet and necks are not visible at a distance, so miss them out completely. You will be amazed at how much more lifelike they look!

Try not to draw figures standing stiffly like tailor's dummies – they will look more lifelike if they are doing something active: carrying bags of shopping, leading dogs or children, looking in a shop window or chatting.

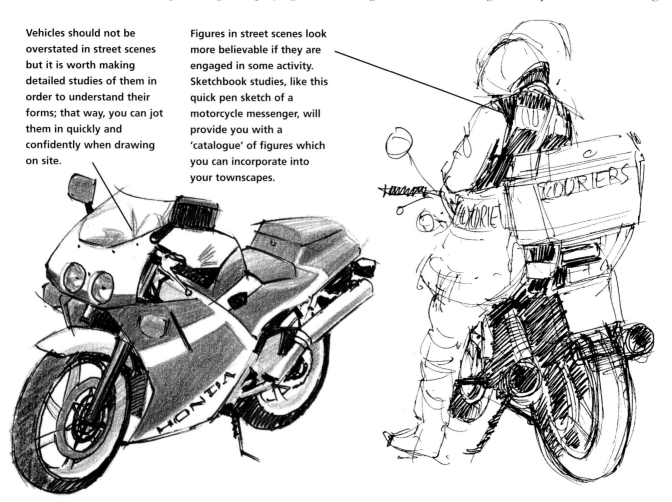

Vehicles should not be overstated in street scenes but it is worth making detailed studies of them in order to understand their forms; that way, you can jot them in quickly and confidently when drawing on site.

Figures in street scenes look more believable if they are engaged in some activity. Sketchbook studies, like this quick pen sketch of a motorcycle messenger, will provide you with a 'catalogue' of figures which you can incorporate into your townscapes.

Figures are an excellent tool for leading the eye into the distance and giving a feeling of space. Try to arrange them in interesting groups with a few individuals here and there. Obviously they will diminish in size the further away they are but their heads should be on the same level (you can see this in the picture on page 87). Check also that they are related in size to the adjacent buildings: they should not be taller than a nearby door, for instance.

Vehicles

The hard outlines of cars, buses and lorries are less easy to integrate into a composition but, as with figures, suggestion is the key: as long as the shapes and proportions are right it is surprising how little detail you can get away with. You don't have to draw every vehicle – one or two are enough to suggest the bustle and activity of a city, and they can be positioned in the distance or middle distance rather than the foreground.

Working from an upper window, balcony or rooftop presents the opportunity to portray townscapes in a way that they are not usually seen: people and traffic look completely different when observed from above.

Most cars have a box-like shape, which makes them relatively easy to draw in perspective. Adding a few vehicles in your composition will help to convey an atmosphere of movement and activity.

Of all the subjects which an artist is likely to tackle, the human figure is undoubtedly the most challenging. If you can learn to draw faces and figures well, then you will be able to draw anything competently. It is not essential to have a thorough knowledge of anatomy in order to draw portraits and figures successfully. What is needed, however, as with any drawing subject, is a keen and analytical eye and a willingness to keep practising, even if your first attempts are unsuccessful.

People and Portraits

Learning to interpret accurately the proportions of the body and at the same time instil a feeling of life into a figure is a real test of the artist's skill. Constant measurement and re-assessment while you work will help to ensure that your drawing is an accurate rendition of your subject, and this chapter offers practical advice on how to measure scale and proportion.

THE HUMAN FIGURE

With a few simple rules as a guide, you will find that drawing the human figure is much less difficult than you might have thought. It's all a matter of keeping things in proportion.

Figure drawing requires a higher degree of accuracy than most subjects. It doesn't really matter if the tree in your landscape drawing is slightly misshapen, but in a figure drawing, if the head is too small or the legs too short, it will be very noticeable.

Proportions of the figure

It is helpful to know the proportions of the 'ideal' figure so that you can use them as a guide to accuracy when drawing people. Most artists use the head as a convenient unit of measurement. In a standing figure, the height of the head fits into the rest of the body approximately seven times. The mid-point is not the waist, as is commonly assumed, but just above the crotch. With the arms by the side, the hands reach halfway down the thighs. The feet are generally about one head length long – a common mistake is to draw them too small. These are useful guidelines but don't use them as a substitute for direct observation: few of us have perfectly proportioned bodies!

The proportions of the body change as we grow and develop. The average adult body is approximately seven heads tall; a young child's body is about five heads tall and an older child's about six heads tall. These proportions provide a useful starting point but you will find that individual sitters often vary slightly from this average.

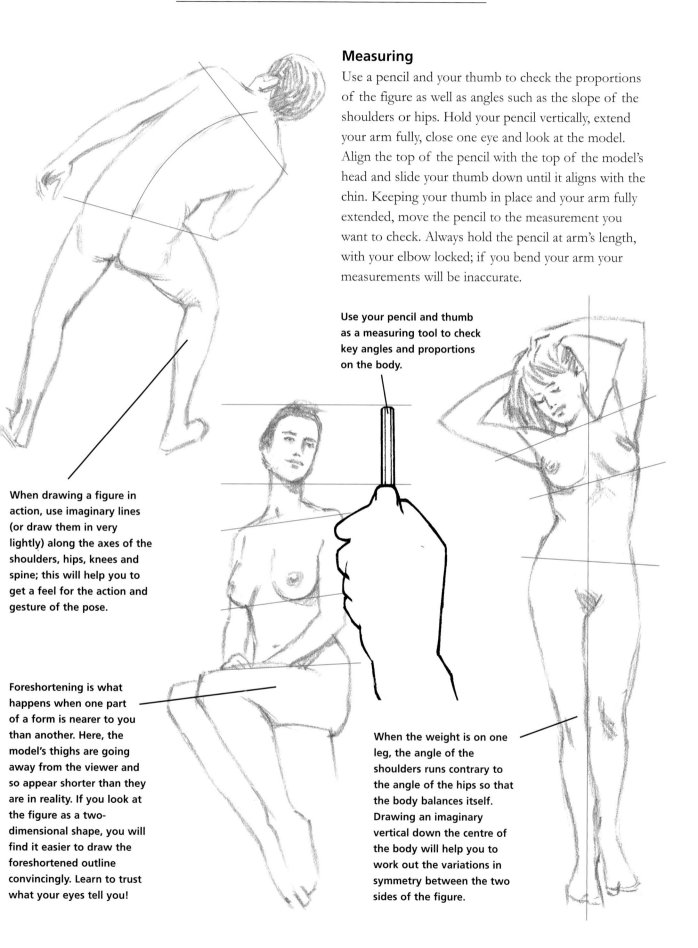

Measuring

Use a pencil and your thumb to check the proportions of the figure as well as angles such as the slope of the shoulders or hips. Hold your pencil vertically, extend your arm fully, close one eye and look at the model. Align the top of the pencil with the top of the model's head and slide your thumb down until it aligns with the chin. Keeping your thumb in place and your arm fully extended, move the pencil to the measurement you want to check. Always hold the pencil at arm's length, with your elbow locked; if you bend your arm your measurements will be inaccurate.

Use your pencil and thumb as a measuring tool to check key angles and proportions on the body.

When drawing a figure in action, use imaginary lines (or draw them in very lightly) along the axes of the shoulders, hips, knees and spine; this will help you to get a feel for the action and gesture of the pose.

Foreshortening is what happens when one part of a form is nearer to you than another. Here, the model's thighs are going away from the viewer and so appear shorter than they are in reality. If you look at the figure as a two-dimensional shape, you will find it easier to draw the foreshortened outline convincingly. Learn to trust what your eyes tell you!

When the weight is on one leg, the angle of the shoulders runs contrary to the angle of the hips so that the body balances itself. Drawing an imaginary vertical down the centre of the body will help you to work out the variations in symmetry between the two sides of the figure.

SKETCHBOOK STUDIES

It is a good idea to get into the habit of carrying a pocket sketchbook around with you, in order to make lots of rapid sketches of figures as often as you can.

Regular sketching is the best way to learn how to portray figures convincingly, so get out and about and sketch people in everyday situations as often as you can. Find a suitable location where people tend to congregate and linger, such as cafés and restaurants, train stations, museums and art galleries. At the beach or in the local park, people walking dogs, playing games or sitting on benches provide ample models. Shops and markets, sports grounds and building sites offer the challenge of sketching moving figures. The possibilities are endless.

Drawing in public places calls for courage and self-confidence, but with a pocket-sized sketchbook and a simple pen or pencil tucked in your pocket, a sketch can be made in a few minutes, even a few seconds, and

Watercolour allows you to capture the vital elements of a scene with rapid strokes and washes, producing a lively interpretation of the subject which could form the basis of a finished painting back at home.

Choose a spot where your subjects are unaware that they are being sketched, allowing you to catch lively expressions and movements.

A journey on public transport need not be boring if you carry your sketchbook with you. Trains, buses and planes are great places for people-watching, and if you manage to draw discreetly and catch people unawares, you can produce marvellous character studies.

31/5/96

blonde hair.

white blouse.

very pale subtle yellow green

black skirt Black Tights

dark beads & filings

Black Shoes.

Grey Sweatshirt pale Blue Jeans

Pubs and bars are an excellent source of characters, expressive gestures and incidental details. This sketch was drawn with waterproof ink and watercolour wash.

A quick, spontaneous sketch can often be more incisive and expressive than a highly finished drawing because it captures the essentials of character and gesture.

Leopard Skin.

Blue Black

it can be done discreetly. You don't have to think in terms of making a finished drawing: a note or two of what you see at a glance, jotted down quickly on the page, is every bit as valid as a 'proper' drawing.

Keep your sketches small and simple. Speed is of the essence, so try to grasp the essentials – the overall shape, posture and action of the figure – at first glance. Don't be discouraged if your initial attempts are inaccurate, or too tight, or unfinished – even the merest scribble is useful in developing your drawing and observational skills. As the speed and volume of your sketches increases, any stiffness in your drawing should disappear and expressing what you see and feel will become increasingly intuitive.

THE FIGURE IN PENCIL

By studying a variety of poses you will soon get a feel for the proportions of the human figure. Pencil is a good medium to start with as it is easily corrected.

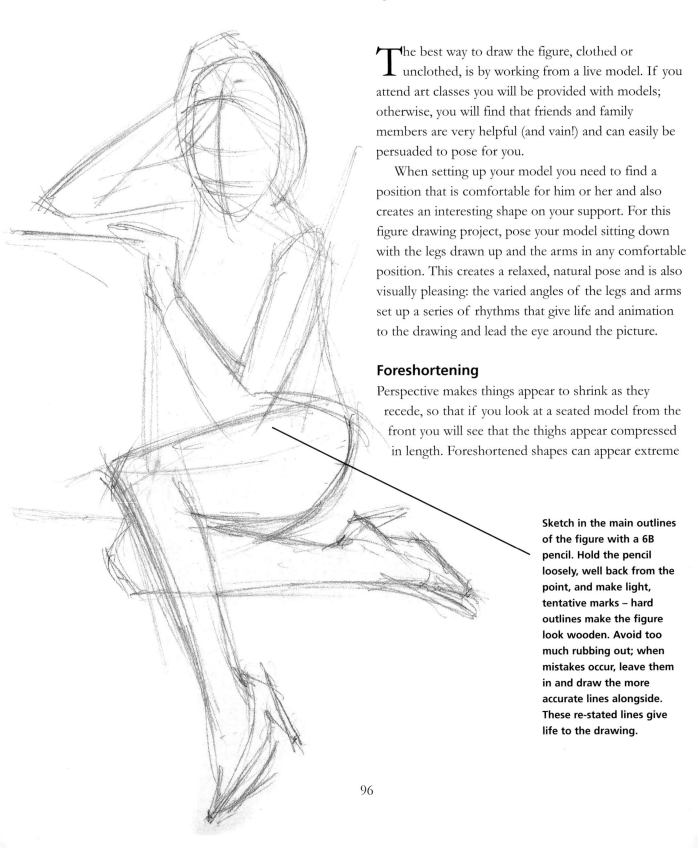

The best way to draw the figure, clothed or unclothed, is by working from a live model. If you attend art classes you will be provided with models; otherwise, you will find that friends and family members are very helpful (and vain!) and can easily be persuaded to pose for you.

When setting up your model you need to find a position that is comfortable for him or her and also creates an interesting shape on your support. For this figure drawing project, pose your model sitting down with the legs drawn up and the arms in any comfortable position. This creates a relaxed, natural pose and is also visually pleasing: the varied angles of the legs and arms set up a series of rhythms that give life and animation to the drawing and lead the eye around the picture.

Foreshortening

Perspective makes things appear to shrink as they recede, so that if you look at a seated model from the front you will see that the thighs appear compressed in length. Foreshortened shapes can appear extreme

Sketch in the main outlines of the figure with a 6B pencil. Hold the pencil loosely, well back from the point, and make light, tentative marks – hard outlines make the figure look wooden. Avoid too much rubbing out; when mistakes occur, leave them in and draw the more accurate lines alongside. These re-stated lines give life to the drawing.

Once you are happy that the outline of the figure is accurate, rub out the guidelines and start to tidy up the drawing – though still avoiding making hard outlines. Indicate the positions of the facial details and the outline of the hair. Start to emphasize the important lines, making them heavier where they project forward and lighter where they recede.

Half-close your eyes so that you can see the areas of light and shadow. Apply loose hatching to the shaded areas of the face and limbs. This will make the figure appear more solid and three-dimensional. Finally, apply more pressure with the pencil to add dark tones to the hair, sweater and shoes.

and you may want to alter them to make them more recognizable. But you must force yourself to draw what you see, not what you know. To help you get the shapes and proportions right, use the pencil-and-thumb method described on page 93. You might also like to make a quick sketch before you begin your drawing

Start by sketching in the overall outline of the figure with fluid lines, making sure that it will fit comfortably on the page. Draw with your whole arm, not just your fingers. Only when you have something resembling the pose should you return to specific areas and start to tighten them up.

THE FIGURE IN WATERCOLOUR

To develop your skills in figure and portrait work, why not start by making informal studies of your family and friends? In this project, quick watercolour washes create an appealing and lifelike portrait.

Informal portraits are the artistic equivalent of a snapshot, in which the subject is dressed casually and adopts a relaxed and natural pose. They can be great fun to do and the result, if successful, is a lively image that captures the personality of the sitter more readily than a formal portrait might.

If possible, persuade a friend or family member to pose for you for a couple of hours at least. This will give you plenty of time to try out different poses and make preliminary sketches. When you have decided on

a pose and your sitter is relaxed and comfortable, give him or her a fixed point to look at, such as a picture on the wall, so that the position of the head and eyes remains constant. Remember that frequent breaks are essential for your sitter. Before a break, use masking tape or chalk to mark the position of feet, hands and elbows on the floor and chair so that he or she can regain, as near as possible, the exact pose after the break.

Give some thought to the position of the figure on the paper. The head should not be so close to the top

Begin with an outline drawing in pencil. You may have to alter and correct the drawing several times before you are ready to paint, so use a soft pencil and draw with light pressure. Avoid too much rubbing out as this spoils the surface of the paper.

Dampen the figure and chair with clean water and brush in the main areas of colour quickly, using as large a brush as you can. Treat the hair as one overall mass, then suggest the curls and tresses with curved strokes.

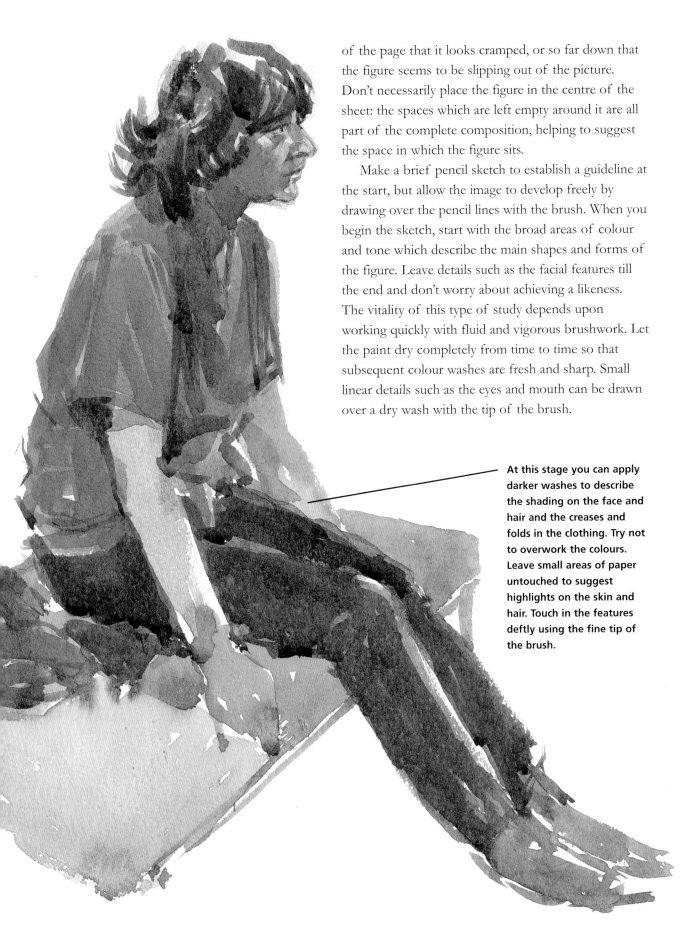

of the page that it looks cramped, or so far down that the figure seems to be slipping out of the picture. Don't necessarily place the figure in the centre of the sheet: the spaces which are left empty around it are all part of the complete composition, helping to suggest the space in which the figure sits.

Make a brief pencil sketch to establish a guideline at the start, but allow the image to develop freely by drawing over the pencil lines with the brush. When you begin the sketch, start with the broad areas of colour and tone which describe the main shapes and forms of the figure. Leave details such as the facial features till the end and don't worry about achieving a likeness. The vitality of this type of study depends upon working quickly with fluid and vigorous brushwork. Let the paint dry completely from time to time so that subsequent colour washes are fresh and sharp. Small linear details such as the eyes and mouth can be drawn over a dry wash with the tip of the brush.

At this stage you can apply darker washes to describe the shading on the face and hair and the creases and folds in the clothing. Try not to overwork the colours. Leave small areas of paper untouched to suggest highlights on the skin and hair. Touch in the features deftly using the fine tip of the brush.

SKETCHING CHILDREN AND BABIES

Sketches and drawings are a wonderful way to capture those precious moments of childhood that are over all too soon. But you have to learn to be 'quick on the draw!'

Drawing young children is always a challenge because they never keep still for long. Start off gently by drawing a child asleep, or absorbed in a favourite book or TV programme. At least you will stand half a chance of getting something down on paper! When you feel brave enough, progress to sketching children on the move. The secret is speed and practice. If you have children at home, keep your drawing materials readily to hand and try to make at least one sketch of them every day. Your pace of drawing will increase and you will begin to develop methods of rapid notation that enable you to catch a fleeting pose or expression.

Children are at their most natural when they are engaged in play and the interaction between them is always interesting. Their obvious enjoyment and absorption can make a fascinating study.

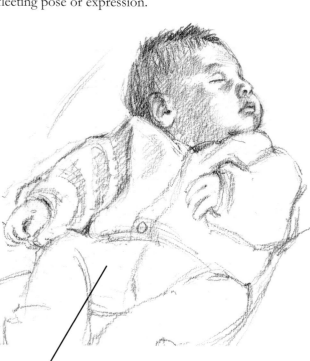

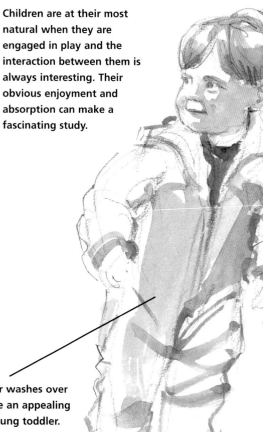

A baby has a very large head in comparison to its body. It has very rounded, large cheeks and the eyes, nose and mouth are crowded into a small area of the face.

Here, delicate watercolour washes over light pencil outlines create an appealing and lifelike sketch of a young toddler. The pose – head turned, one leg slightly raised – implies movement and energy.

A light, sensitive touch with a soft pencil conveys the soft, rounded cheeks and delicate features of these young girls. Try to match your drawing style to the nature of the subject: light, tentative strokes will convey childlike qualities better than hard, continuous outlines.

These simple pencil sketches capture the charm and innocence of young children at play. Making quick, sketchy drawings of moving children helps to develop your speed and confidence so that you are better able to capture something of the energy and vitality of your subjects.

As children move about and play, make several sketches on a single sheet and dart from one to the other. Put down your impressions with simple, unfussy strokes and concentrate on the outline shapes and gestures of the figures – don't worry unduly about details such as faces and hands.

Selecting a medium

To capture the charm and innocence of children, and their energy and enthusiasm, you will need a medium that is both rapid and sensitive. Soft pencil is a good 'instant' medium that can also be smudged with a finger for soft tones. Very quick sketches can be made by smudging soft pastel or charcoal to catch the overall shape of the pose, then drawing in the details with the point of the stick. Gentle watercolour washes are perfect for delicate sketches of babies and young children. The contours of the face and body are much softer in children than in adults, so modelling should be kept broad and simple.

FIGURES IN ACTION

Drawing people who are moving may seem daunting at first. But with practice you will develop an instinctive 'shorthand' of quick strokes and flowing lines that convey dynamism, energy and life.

There are two approaches to drawing the figure in action: movement can be expressed by depicting the action at or just after its peak. Look at images in the sports pages and note how the photographer captures the peak moment in a stride, a kick, a swing or a reach.

One way of breaking yourself in to the process of capturing movement is to ask someone to model repeated movements for you while you make quick sketches. Because the actions are repeated, you can wait for a limb to adopt a similar pose perhaps several times, each occasion giving you the chance to refine and correct your drawing.

The second approach to capturing movement is to make the drawing itself convey an impression of action and mobility through the character of the drawn marks. Don't try to 'fix' the figure on the paper with a solid outline as this tends to freeze the action. Instead, you

In this pastel drawing, the dynamic shapes formed by the limbs and the directional lines describing the runner's hair convey speed and agility.

Take your sketchbook along to a dance class or party and make lots of speedy scribble drawings of people dancing. Use a fast medium such as a graphite stick and concentrate on the shapes of the figures, ignoring detail.

102

will need to develop a repertoire of fast, instinctive marks that suggest mobility. Sweeping, gestural marks, drawn with speed, imply action, as do broken, nervous lines. The calligraphic quality of lines that swell and taper as they follow the form suggests a changing balance of weight and direction that implies mobility. Movement can also be suggested by softening or fading out parts that are moving, such as the legs. When using charcoal or chalk, for instance, use your finger to blend and blur some of the outlines.

This drawing conveys the sudden spurt of a rugby player breaking into a run. The forward thrust of the pose is captured in the vigorously hatched diagonal lines, the broken, agitated quality of these lines suggesting force and energy. The shifting weight of the body is emphasized by the outward thrust of the player's left arm.

Before starting to draw a moving figure, spend some time just sitting and watching. Concentrate all your attention on the action of the figure and how the head, limbs and torso are positioned. Notice how the balance of the whole body changes during the action.

DRAWING THE HEAD

When drawing portraits, you will find it easier to achieve an accurate likeness if you have an understanding of the physical structure of the head and the proportions of the face.

Before tackling an actual portrait drawing, practise rendering some simple head shapes and learning how to position the features correctly in relation to the head. The basic form of the head is determined by the bony structure of the skull. This can be visualized as an upside-down egg shape with the wider end representing the top of the head. Having established the shape of the head, you can position the features, and here the 'rule of halves' is a useful guide. First, draw a vertical line down the centre of the head to mark the position

Carry a small sketchbook with you at all times and make quick sketches of faces you see around you. People dozing on the train will be unaware of your scrutiny and you can practise drawing heads tilted at different angles.

The facial features occupy a surprisingly small area of the head. It is important to position them correctly in order to achieve a good likeness. Use the rule of halves as a rough guide to the positioning of the facial features.

of the nose and the centre of the lips. Then draw a horizontal line across the centre of the head: this marks the position of the eyes and from here it is easy to gauge the eyebrow line. Sketch a line midway between the eyebrow line and the tip of the chin in order to find the position of the base of the nose. Then draw a line midway between the base of the nose and the tip of the chin to find the line of the lower lip.

Now you can sketch in the features. The gap between the eyes is approximately the width of an eye. The ears line up between the eyebrows and the tip of the nose. The hairline normally sits about one-third of the way down from the crown of the head.

Do bear in mind that the rule of halves is intended only as a guide to the 'average' face. Each individual is different and it is the variations from the norm that give a face its distinctive character: your sitter may have a long nose or a large chin, for instance. Check proportions and relationships by measuring with your pencil (see pages 92-93).

When the head is tilted upwards, downwards or to one side, the features appear foreshortened. As with the foreshortened figure, it can be difficult to accept these distortions until you learn to look at them logically.

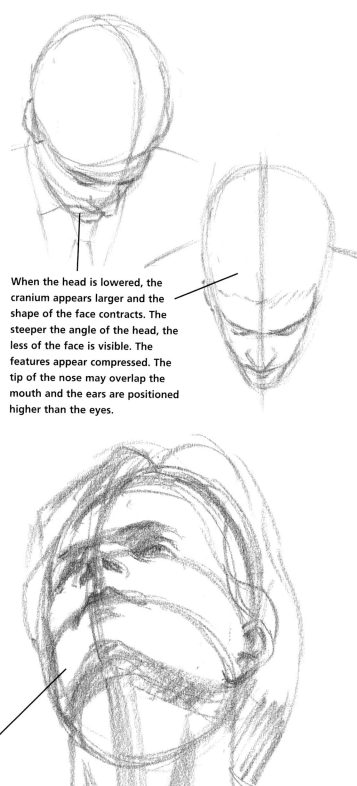

When the head is lowered, the cranium appears larger and the shape of the face contracts. The steeper the angle of the head, the less of the face is visible. The features appear compressed. The tip of the nose may overlap the mouth and the ears are positioned higher than the eyes.

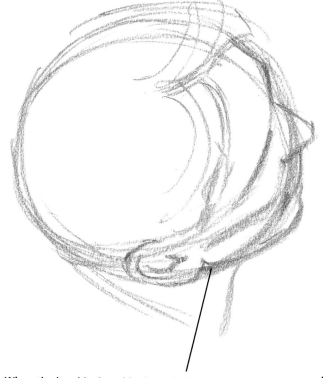

When the head is tipped backwards the eyes and nose appear much closer together. Notice how the facial features follow the curve of the underlying skull.

105

A PORTRAIT IN PENCIL

*In this first portrait drawing project, you will discover how to convey
an individual's facial features and how to build up a sense of form
and volume with pencil lines and shading.*

When drawing a portrait, you need to think like a sculptor and work from the general to the particular. Start by blocking in the main lights and shadows that model the face. Once the structure is in place, you can progress to looking for the shapes within the shapes, and then further breaking down the subtle planes and patches of tone that define the features. In pencil, form is modelled by building up the density of

Draw the outline of the head with a 4B pencil. Measure the proportions with your pencil and lightly mark in guidelines to position the features. As the head is turned slightly to the left, the centre line is slightly to the left of the drawing. Briefly sketch in the features.

Begin modelling the head with light hatching lines. Alter the direction of the strokes so that they follow the curves of the face. This establishes a clear distinction between the light and shadow areas and already there is a strong sense of form and volume.

hatching in the darker areas and leaving the lightest areas blank. This process of reduction allows you to see the head as a whole and not just a collection of separate parts. After all, a sculptor doesn't take a chunk of clay and carefully chip out a nose here, an eye there. He begins with the large planes and masses and once he has got these right he works up to the details.

Avoid the temptation to draw the eyes, nose and mouth with continuous outlines; use sensitive, searching strokes and 'chisel out' the forms with tonal shading to make them appear an integral part of the face. Shade under the brow to show how the eyes are recessed. The mouth is soft and mobile; it does not have an outline but is defined by light and shadow. The upper lip appears darker than the lower one, which catches more light. The nose is a form projecting from the front of the face – draw it by indicating planes at either side and underneath.

Develop the stronger darks within the shadow areas – the eye sockets and eyes, the nostrils, the upper lip and the shadow cast by the nose, the shadow under the neck, and the cleft of the chin. Leave white paper for the highlights where the light catches the model's forehead, nose and chin. Give the hair more volume with strong directional strokes. Finally, hatch in some shadow tone behind the head.

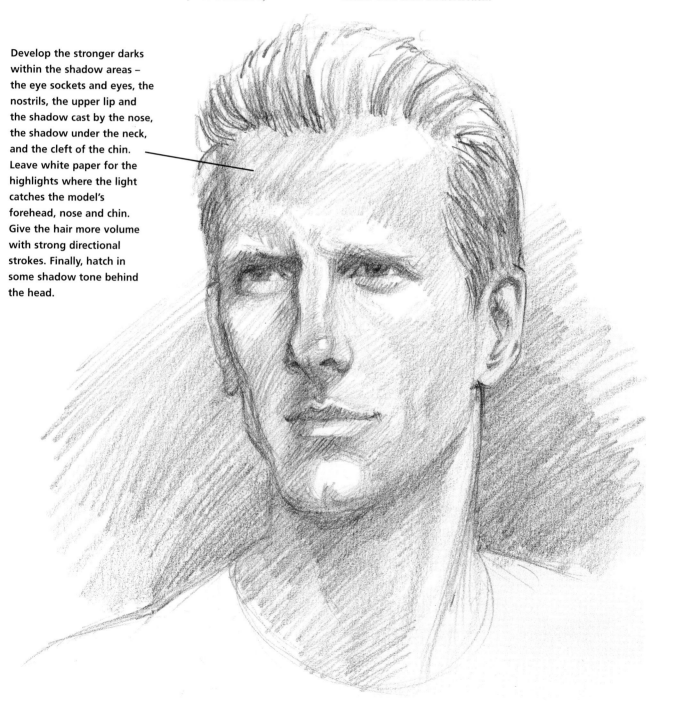

A PORTRAIT IN PASTEL

*It is essential in a portrait to place the features correctly and then
make sure that the basic shapes of mouth, nose and eyes and the
outline of the head and jaw are as close to your model as possible.*

When drawing a portrait, the beginner tends to concentrate on the eyes, nose and mouth. But if the features are not correctly positioned at the outset, there is little chance of achieving a good likeness of the sitter. Each human being has facial proportions unique to themselves, which is why we are able to recognize someone from a distance. These basic proportions are the most essential elements in capturing a likeness. Start by establishing the dominant angles, masses and planes and block in the main lights and shadows that model the face and head. As you draw, look and look again, checking one feature in relation to another and comparing angles and proportions. Once the structure is in place, you can progress to refining the features.

After studying the shape of the head, draw the outline, marking the area of the hair and the position of the eyes, nose and mouth. Use a medium-toned pastel for this preliminary sketch and don't be afraid to make corrections to your drawing.

Now you can start to build up basic areas of tone. Use your pastels to create areas of light and dark without worrying too much about the actual colours you are using. A darker pastel will make a frame for your portrait and can be used to build up details.

Try to keep your shading fresh and lively – the overall effect is more important than trying to capture every 'photographic' detail.

Your portrait will soon start to take shape as you add and blend colours. Lines have been added to emphasize the strands of hair, the eyes, nose and mouth, and generally to enhance the overall quality of the drawing.

Work with a limited range of colours rather than trying to use every pastel in your box. Four different tones will give you plenty of scope.

The materials for this project are coloured pastels in four different colour tones ranging from cream to dark brown, on slightly textured white paper. The paper shows through the pastel marks across the drawing, creating the highlights on the face and adding luminosity to the skin tones. The limited range of colours allows you to build up the image with simple blocks of tone but they can be laid over each other and blended to provide smooth transitions from light to dark.

A PORTRAIT IN WATERCOLOUR

Watercolour is an excellent medium for spontaneous, informal portrait studies. Its fluidity and translucency are perfectly matched to the subject, bringing out the delicate, living qualities of skin and hair.

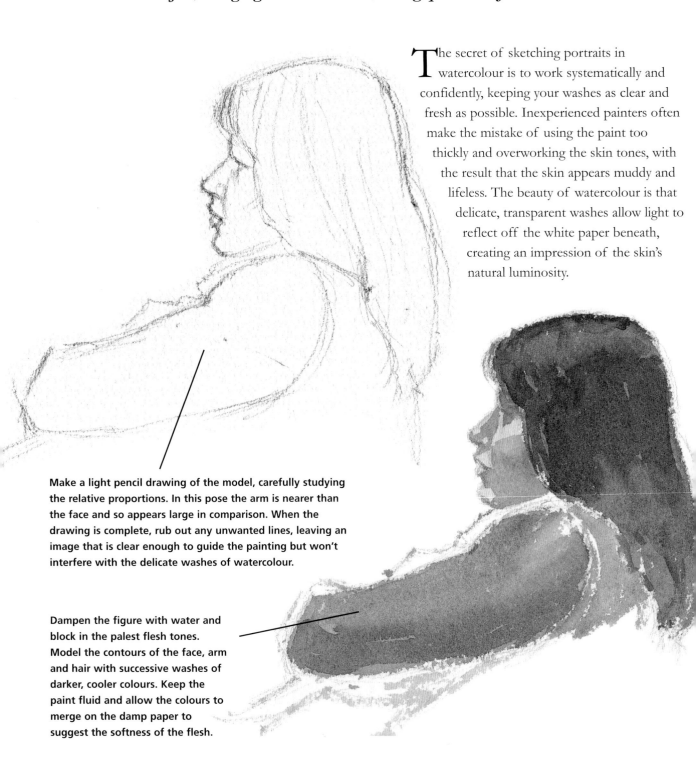

The secret of sketching portraits in watercolour is to work systematically and confidently, keeping your washes as clear and fresh as possible. Inexperienced painters often make the mistake of using the paint too thickly and overworking the skin tones, with the result that the skin appears muddy and lifeless. The beauty of watercolour is that delicate, transparent washes allow light to reflect off the white paper beneath, creating an impression of the skin's natural luminosity.

Make a light pencil drawing of the model, carefully studying the relative proportions. In this pose the arm is nearer than the face and so appears large in comparison. When the drawing is complete, rub out any unwanted lines, leaving an image that is clear enough to guide the painting but won't interfere with the delicate washes of watercolour.

Dampen the figure with water and block in the palest flesh tones. Model the contours of the face, arm and hair with successive washes of darker, cooler colours. Keep the paint fluid and allow the colours to merge on the damp paper to suggest the softness of the flesh.

In keeping with traditional watercolour practice, always start with very pale, diluted colours and gradually strengthen the tones with successive washes laid one over the other. It is important to keep the colours bright and fresh: you need to use plenty of clean water and rinse your brushes thoroughly after each colour application. Try not to 'muddy' the image with too many colours and keep reworking to a minimum to maintain the delicacy of the washes.

Warm and cool colours

The skin appears lighter and warmer in the prominent, light-struck areas, such as the cheeks and forehead, and darker and cooler in the shadow areas. Because warm colours appear to advance and cool colours to recede, you can use these warm and cool contrasts to model the contours of the face and figure, much as a sculptor pushes and pulls a block of clay. In this portrait, for instance, notice the warm yellows on the cheek, the chin and the bridge of the nose and the subtle hints of cool blue in the shadows of the face and arm.

Apply your colours with confidence and do not attempt to tidy up the loose brush strokes too much – the portrait will look much more lively if you allow some of the brush marks and ragged edges to show rather than blending them neatly together.

Strengthen the colours over the whole image, developing the structure of the face and arm with a series of overlapping washes. Define the tresses of hair with curving brush strokes, letting the pale underwash show through to suggest highlights and individual wisps of hair. Define the eye and mouth with dark colour applied with the tip of the brush.

111

Animals and birds are sometimes frustrating but always fascinating subjects to draw. Their feathers, scales and fur provide a wealth of patterns and textures to explore with a range of media and techniques. Recording their characteristic behaviours, their gestures and movements, will test your skills of observation and mark-making.

Animals and Birds

Drawing animals and birds presents a problem similar to that of drawing young children – they cannot be asked to pose for you, so you will have to rely on preliminary sketches and a good background knowledge of the underlying structure of the animal. Start by drawing your own pet, which is more likely to keep still for you. If you find that you develop an interest in this subject, you can go on to study the animals and birds on farms, in zoos and in the wild.

STARTING WITH SIMPLE SHAPES

Just as students are sometimes taught to base the human figure on simple geometric forms – cylinders, cubes and spheres – this same principle can be used to capture an animal's basic body structure.

Drawing birds and animals requires no special knowledge of their anatomy. Observation is the key to success, plus an awareness of form and structure.

All animals and birds can be visualized as a series of simple, interlocking geometric shapes – circles, ovals, triangles and rectangles. This method provides you with a simple way of recording the overall shape of an animal's body, the position of the limbs and the angles at which they meet the body. Practise by drawing lots of simple animal shapes like the ones below. Use cheap newsprint rather than expensive drawing paper as it is less inhibiting to draw on. Choose a medium which

provides a fluid yet precise line that skates easily over the paper surface – soft pencil, felt-tip or ballpoint pen.

Start by drawing animals from photographs and progress to drawing your own pet, if you have one. Look for the simple underlying shapes: from the side, a cat's head forms a roughly ovoid shape and the ears are small elongated triangles. A dog's head fits into a square or hexagonal shape, depending on the breed, and the body is shaped like a kidney bean. Once you are familiar with the basic shapes of animals, you will find it easier to sketch them from life, with fluid lines and rhythmic gestures which capture their grace and movement.

Simple outline drawings like these are fun to create. They show how it is possible to draw the basic body structure of any animal, large or small, by seeing it as a collection of interlocking geometric shapes. Side views are the simplest to start with.

Treat each part of the body as a single shape – an elongated oval for a head, perhaps, and a series of circles and ovoid shapes for the belly and haunches. Then draw the legs, looking for the correct angles. Practise drawing these shapes until you can do them easily from memory.

115

CATS AND DOGS

*What better way to embark on the pleasures of drawing animals
than to sketch your own pet cat or dog? They make good models as
their movements are predictable, allowing regular occasions for study.*

The advantage of drawing family pets is that they are always around and you can make studies of them sleeping (cats are particularly good at this), eating or gazing out of the window.

Start by sketching your cat or dog sleeping. This gives you a chance to learn about structure and proportions, which will enable you to draw a moving animal quickly and accurately. Next, try sketching your pet while grooming; it will remain fairly stationary but perform a series of repeated movements, which will allow you to record the rhythmic grace of the pose. Have several sketches of different poses on the go at once, and dart around the page as your subject shifts position. This is quite a challenge but you should end up with a page of interesting studies. And you can supplement your sketches with photographs; these are useful for catching active moments but it's not a good idea to slavishly copy from them as they tend to flatten form and reduce detail. Working from direct observation will give you much livelier drawings.

The wiry, long-haired coat of this Border collie is depicted by making the pencil strokes follow the direction of the hairs.

Proportions are important In capturing the individuality of your pet. The big ears, long tail and gangly limbs tell us that this is a pup.

Let sleeping dogs lie – while you move around them and quickly sketch them from different angles!

Form and structure

Try not to labour over the details. Basic proportions, like the relationships between eyes, nose and ears, are more important initially, as are the size of the head in relation to the body, the volume of the legs and their distance apart, and the overall posture. You might find it easier to start by reducing the body to a series of simple geometric shapes (see page 114). A dog's torso, for instance, is shaped rather like a kidney bean, while the head can be treated as an oval with a flattened cylinder for the muzzle. The more sinuous body of a cat forms a series of circles and ovals, with triangles for the ears. Once you've established the basic structure you can refine the shapes and apply the surface details.

This portrait of a tabby cat is worked in soft graphite pencil. The fur is described with a mixture of tonal shading and detailed textural lines. The eyes are the key to the character and expression of an animal. This applies particularly to cats, whose eyes are such a prominent feature. Start your drawing by checking the size and position of the eyes in relation to the other features of the head.

Watercolour is a good medium for conveying the texture of fur if you simplify the furry texture into broad areas of tone rather than attempting to paint each hair. Apply quick, directional brush strokes over an almost-dry underwash to suggest the thick, rug-like fur on the dog's body.

FUR, FEATHERS AND SCALES

The textures, colours and patterns of fur, feathers and scales is a
rewarding area of study when drawing animals. Try to find marks
that will represent them with conviction but without overstatement.

When you are drawing animals and birds you'll find that their patterns and markings can help to describe the underlying form. The stripes of a tiger or a tabby cat, for instance, follow the contours of the body and give it a feeling of solidity. Your first priority, however, is to get down the structure and proportions of the body. Only when you have got the shape and pose right should you start to tackle details and patterns.

It is essential to find a quick, shorthand way of describing an animal's texture or coat pattern. If you try to draw every spot, stripe, hair or feather your drawings will look lifeless and overworked. Observe where the most distinctive markings are and use them to emphasize the shape of the animal in key places such as around the head, shoulders and rump. The eye fills in the gaps, so that a few carefully placed marks are read as a complete pattern or group of hairs.

When drawing the scaly skin of reptiles, a feel for the rhythm of the markings will be more characteristic than the minute reproduction of every detail.

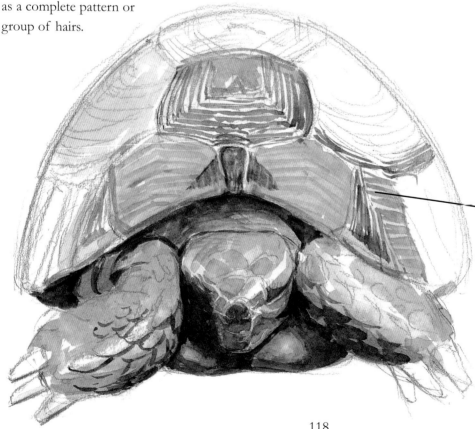

The complex whorls and ridges on a tortoise's shell are a delight. However, you don't have to reproduce each individual scale. In this study, watercolour washes were used to suggest the patterns with a 'lost and found' quality that implies their continuation around the creature's form.

Be expressive with your mark-making to bring out the character of a texture. Short fur can be imitated with hatched lines, the tonal gradations across the body built up by varying the density and pressure of the marks. Draw animals with long, smooth hair using broad areas of tone with occasional lines to suggest the rhythms of its fall. Pay attention also to the shadows and highlights on the fur or feathers as they help to describe the structure of the body beneath.

Coloured pencils were used here to portray the hamster's sleek, velvety, colourful fur with short, fine lines that follow the contours of the form. The tiny highlights on the eye are important in conveying their brightness.

A black Conté pencil held on its side produces soft tones that describe the sleek, smooth and muscular forms of rabbits. Working on a coarse-textured paper helps to give a suggestion of softness to the coat.

Mice, hamsters and gerbils are lively little animals. The speed and suddenness of their movements makes them hard to draw – you just have to sketch rapidly as they skitter about. Pen and colour wash lends itself to the quick approach demanded, and to painting the subtle variations of colour and tone on the animal's body.

119

ON THE FARM

Animals lend scale and interest to landscape drawings and you'll find that studies of farm animals collected in a sketchbook will provide a useful resource that can be dipped into when required.

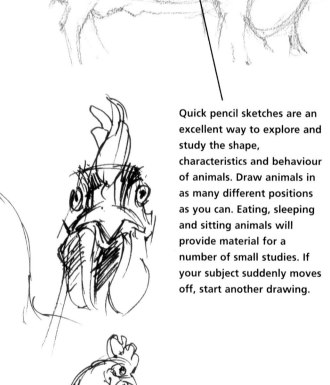

If sketching your pet at home has awakened your interest in drawing animals, you may wish to try your hand at drawing semi-domesticated animals on farms. Even urban dwellers will probably have access to a city farm or children's zoo, where horses, pigs, deer, chickens and ducks can be viewed at close quarters.

Farm animals make good 'models' as they are usually more placid than wild animals, but they do move around enough to keep you on your toes! Horses, sheep and cows tend to move relatively slowly and repeat characteristic poses and this gives you an opportunity to understand the motion and translate it

Quick pencil sketches are an excellent way to explore and study the shape, characteristics and behaviour of animals. Draw animals in as many different positions as you can. Eating, sleeping and sitting animals will provide material for a number of small studies. If your subject suddenly moves off, start another drawing.

Have several sketches of different poses on the go at once and dart around the page as the animal shifts position. This is quite a challenge but you should end up with a page of interesting studies. Superimposing the sketches has the interesting effect of bringing your paper to life.

onto your paper. Try working on a whole sheet of sketches at once; if the animal moves in the middle of a sketch, no matter – start a new one on the same page. The chances are that it will return to a similar position and you can then continue with the first sketch. With each drawing you make, your knowledge and confidence will increase.

Introduce variety into your sketches. Make group studies as well as individual ones – mothers and calves, a gaggle of geese – and, if possible, make in-depth studies of heads and faces. Note how herds of cows and flocks of sheep often face in the same direction when grazing, and look for attractive groupings where some animals are standing, some lying down.

Action will make your pictures more interesting and there is always some activity happening on a farm. Daily routines such as milking, feeding, grooming and so on give you the chance to depict the interaction between the farm animals, people and their surroundings.

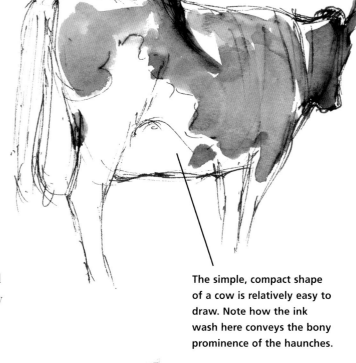

The simple, compact shape of a cow is relatively easy to draw. Note how the ink wash here conveys the bony prominence of the haunches.

Most farm animals are naturally inquisitive and will come up to you and stare; take advantage of this to practise drawing foreshortened poses!

This in-depth study of a bull's head displays a finely controlled use of hatching. Coloured pencils are similar to watercolour in that you have to work from dark to light, leaving areas of white paper to stand for the highlights.

SHAPES AND RHYTHMS

The essence of drawing animals and birds from life is immediacy.
Choose your medium accordingly. Pencil, charcoal, felt-tips and
crayons are ideal because they enable you to sketch quickly.

Drawing animals isn't easy, and sometimes the anxiety we feel when trying to capture a moving subject is evident in rather tight, rigid drawings. But animals are built for sprinting, stretching, leaping and pouncing; their bodies are lithe and full of latent energy, even in repose. So don't freeze up – free up!

Try sketching animals on large sheets of inexpensive paper and draw with your elbow and shoulder as well as your wrist. Get your pencil moving and make fast, fluid, gestural strokes in response to the rhythms of the animal's body. Vary the speed and rhythm of the lines so as to convey a sense of energy and vitality; let them taper or break as they describe a receding form, and give them an emphatic swell on curved shapes.

Concentrate on shapes and postures rather than anatomical accuracy. Your subjects will probably be moving so quickly that there will be no time to worry about details! Choose a medium that glides over the surface of the paper, allowing you to render an outline or capture a gesture with speed. Soft pencil is the most convenient medium for sketching fast-moving animals, but felt-tips, charcoal and graphite sticks are also good.

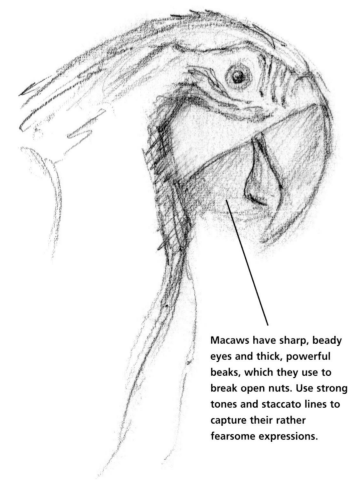

Macaws have sharp, beady eyes and thick, powerful beaks, which they use to break open nuts. Use strong tones and staccato lines to capture their rather fearsome expressions.

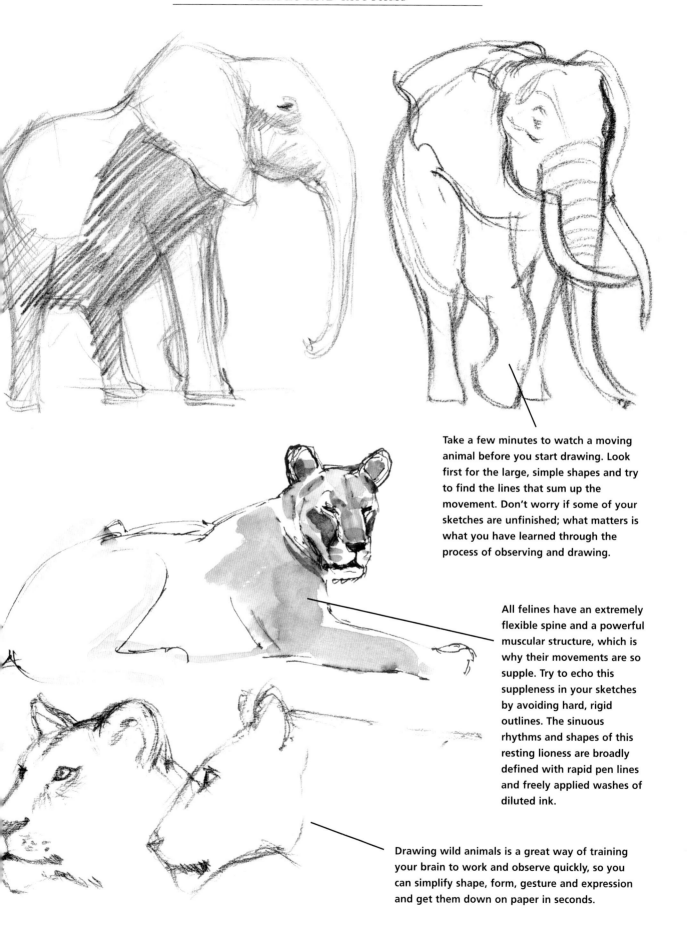

Take a few minutes to watch a moving animal before you start drawing. Look first for the large, simple shapes and try to find the lines that sum up the movement. Don't worry if some of your sketches are unfinished; what matters is what you have learned through the process of observing and drawing.

All felines have an extremely flexible spine and a powerful muscular structure, which is why their movements are so supple. Try to echo this suppleness in your sketches by avoiding hard, rigid outlines. The sinuous rhythms and shapes of this resting lioness are broadly defined with rapid pen lines and freely applied washes of diluted ink.

Drawing wild animals is a great way of training your brain to work and observe quickly, so you can simplify shape, form, gesture and expression and get them down on paper in seconds.

123

SKETCHING AT THE ZOO

Zoos and safari parks offer us a rare opportunity to sketch and draw exotic wildlife. Here, the city-bound sketcher can record on paper the weird and the wonderful, the funny and the ferocious.

Spend a day at the zoo and make lots of quick sketches of fast-moving animals as well as longer studies of creatures at rest. It will help your sketches enormously if you take a few minutes to watch your subject moving about before you begin drawing. Zoo animals often repeat patterns of behaviour – some frequently. The big cats, for example, tend to pace back and forth inside their enclosure: this regular, cyclical motion gives you the chance to observe a given posture a number of times and get it down quickly on paper. Always start by getting down the bulk and proportions of the animal and its posture with fluid, searching lines.

Details such as fur markings and facial features should only be added once you are satisfied that the overall shape is correct.

While the animals are confined, the human animals are not, and at times an artist at work can feel like a zoo exhibit, being gawped at by curious onlookers! However, with a small sketchbook you should remain relatively unobtrusive, and you will soon learn to ignore people and get on with the work in hand. Hardback sketchbooks with rigid binding are more practical than the spiral-bound variety, being easier to handle and enabling you to work across the spread of two pages.

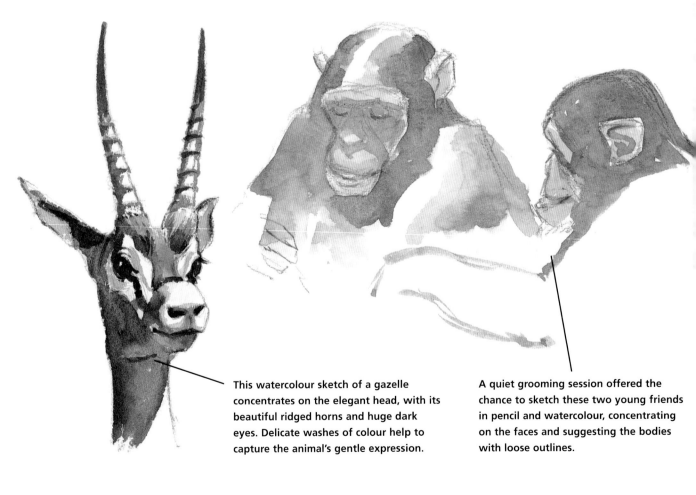

This watercolour sketch of a gazelle concentrates on the elegant head, with its beautiful ridged horns and huge dark eyes. Delicate washes of colour help to capture the animal's gentle expression.

A quiet grooming session offered the chance to sketch these two young friends in pencil and watercolour, concentrating on the faces and suggesting the bodies with loose outlines.

The expression on this Siberian tiger's face is dignified and unfaltering. Always search out the structure of the head before drawing the facial features. The beautiful markings are important in indicating the shape of the head and shoulders and coloured pencils enable you to draw these with softness and precision. For a detailed study like this, photographs can be a useful back-up to your sketches.

STUDIES OF BIRDS

Patient observation is the key to success when drawing birds. Make multiple sketchbook studies of birds on the ground and in flight, recording the characteristic shapes and markings of different species.

No matter where you live, there are always birds to sketch – in gardens, parks, forests and farmland, as well as in zoos and urban farms. If you haven't tried drawing birds before, however, you may prefer to 'get your hand in' by working from photographs in wildlife magazines and natural history books initially. Making detailed studies of stuffed specimens in a natural history museum will enable you to examine form, colour and pattern closely and discover the best marks to use to describe the markings of the feathers and details such as beaks and claws.

All of this groundwork will pay dividends when you progress to drawing living birds in their natural surroundings. A wide variety of birds can be found in your own garden, especially if you encourage them with

The magnificent head of an eagle is worthy of detailed study. Layers of finely worked coloured pencil lines suggest the density of the head feathers.

A sheet of studies of a bird drawn from different angles will acquaint you not only with its shape and movements but also with its temperament and character. Here, quick sketches of the overall shape are supplemented with more in-depth studies of the head in colour.

a regular supply of food. While the birds are feeding you will have an excellent opportunity to sketch their gestures and movements and observe their fascinating behaviour. Watch out for preening birds, too: preening is often accompanied by wing, tail and leg-stretching – actions which result in some delightful poses. Concentrate on shape and movement rather than detail.

A quick monochrome sketch in brown pencil establishes bulk, form and wing patterns with a few simple lines. The unfinished head is deliberately left in to give a sense of the bird's rapid head movements as it devours its prey.

It is possible to capture the formidable beauty of a large bird of prey in a zoo, where the confined situation encourages the birds to sit still for long periods of time. Watercolour is a suitable medium for recording detailed impressions, conveying the bird's bulk and the structure of feathers with delicacy and freedom.

When sketching birds in the wild you won't have time to labour over a single drawing. Take the opportunity instead to make several quick, animated studies, searching for the characteristic outlines and gestures of your subjects. These sketches of seagulls were made with a mixture of dip pen and sepia ink, white pastel and coloured pencil on tinted paper. Composite sheets like this are invaluable for future reference.

INDEX